PENGUIN BOOKS

Victoria

Jane Ridley is Professor of Modern History at Buckingham University, where she teaches a course on biography. Her previous books include *The Young Disraeli*; a study of Edwin Lutyens, *The Architect and his Wife,* which won the 2003 Duff Cooper Prize; and the best-selling *Bertie: A Life of Edward VII.* A Fellow of the Royal Society for Literature, Ridley writes for the *Spectator* and other newspapers, and has appeared on radio and several television documentaries. She lives in London and Scotland.

JANE RIDLEY

Victoria
Queen, Matriarch, Empress

PENGUIN BOOKS

PENGUIN BOOKS

UK | USA | Canada | Ireland | Australia
India | New Zealand | South Africa

Penguin Books is part of the Penguin Random House group of companies
whose addresses can be found at global.penguinrandomhouse.com.

First published by Allen Lane 2015
First published in Penguin Books 2018
001

Set in 9.5/13.5 pt Sabon LT Std
Typeset by Jouve (UK), Milton Keynes
Printed and bound in Great Britain by Clays Ltd, Elcograf S.p.A.

ISBN: 978-0-141-98731-6

www.greenpenguin.co.uk

MIX
Paper from
responsible sources
FSC® C018179

Penguin Random House is committed to a
sustainable future for our business, our readers
and our planet. This book is made from Forest
Stewardship Council® certified paper.

Contents

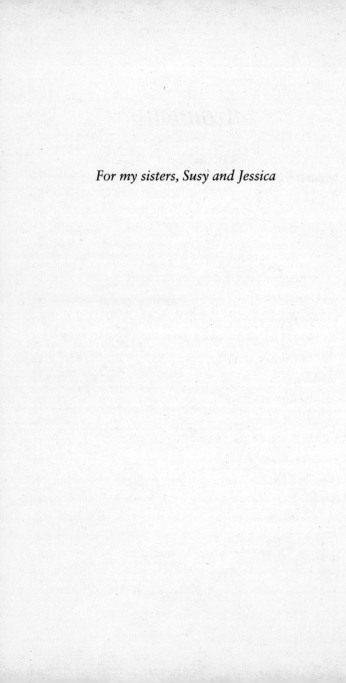

For my sisters, Susy and Jessica

Introduction

'It is one o'clock and all, all is over!' wrote Queen Victoria on 23 December 1861.[1] Wearing deepest black and a locket of Albert's hair round her neck, the queen sat at her desk at Osborne, her Italianate palace on the Isle of Wight. At Windsor, mourned by his red-eyed household and sobbing sons, Albert's coffin was lowered into the vault of the British kings in the silent gloom of St George's Chapel. His death aged forty-two was as unexpected as it was annihilating for the queen. Howling with grief, bursting into paroxysms of uncontrollable weeping and tortured by sleepless nights, she had been forced to leave her husband's body and hide at Osborne. 'My life as I considered it is gone, past, closed!'[2] 'To the Queen it is like <u>death</u> in life!', she wrote.[3] To the foreign secretary she wrote of her '<u>utter desolation, darkness</u> and <u>loneliness</u>'.[4]

Victoria ordered the Blue Room at Windsor where Albert had died to be photographed and kept as a shrine exactly as he had left it, 'even to an open pocket handkerchief on the sofa'.[5] The same rituals were performed at Osborne. Some worried about her sanity. But the queen remained clear-headed. She was sure of one thing: she would not abdicate. On the day after the funeral she told her uncle, King Leopold of Belgium, that her work in life would be to make '<u>his</u> wishes ... <u>his</u> plans ... <u>my law</u>!'. 'I am <u>also</u>

<u>determined</u> that <u>no one</u> person, may <u>he</u> be ever so good ...
is to lead or dictate <u>to me</u>.'[6] She would rule alone.

The death of Prince Albert was a hinge, splitting the life
of the forty-two-year-old Victoria into two halves. The first
part was almost a fairy story, or so it seemed. The unhappy
princess, kept virtually a prisoner by her mother, had succeeded as queen four weeks after her eighteenth birthday.
Her court was a Camelot, famed for its youth and gaiety.
But, fatally ignorant of politics, Victoria was dancing to
disaster. From this she was rescued by her marriage to
Albert, in one of the great love matches of history. This is
the romantic narrative of Victoria's life, reprised in films
such as *The Young Victoria* (2009). It is the story with
which we are most familiar. Victoria's early life has become
a media industry, a spin-off from Jane Austen Inc.

The second half of Victoria's life is strangely obscure. The
Widow of Windsor hid from her people for forty years,
and she has managed to elude her biographers too. As
Lytton Strachey wrote, 'For her biographer, there is a darkness over the latter half of [Victoria's] long career ... With
Albert's death a veil descends.'[7] Defeated by this darkness –
and by the sheer weight of material – her biographers
Monica Charlot (1991) and Cecil Woodham-Smith (1972)
abandoned ship in 1861. Elizabeth Longford (1964) was
the first biographer to steer a course through the volumin-
ous archives of Victoria's life post-Albert. But only A. N.
Wilson (2014), her most recent biographer, has shifted the
focus to the second half of Victoria's life, suggesting that
Albert's death was a sort of liberation, allowing her to real-
ize her true self after a painful struggle with her demons.

My first in-depth encounter with Queen Victoria came when I was writing a biography of her son, Bertie, later King Edward VII. I was astonished by the way she treated her children. Letters and reprimands rained down, penned in Victoria's emphatic hand, heavily underlined, her nib digging deep into the paper. As a parent, Victoria seemed extraordinarily unsympathetic, especially to twenty-first-century eyes. It struck me that she had displayed all the characteristics of an angry, unloving mother during the time that was supposedly the happiest of her life – her marriage to Albert. Perhaps the marriage was not so perfect after all. Perhaps the glossy Hollywood image of *The Young Victoria* is largely a myth. And Victoria's later years, shrouded in mystery, are far more interesting than the 'we are not amused' cliché implies. There is, for a start, the question of how the diminutive and invisible queen became in her old age one of the most powerful women in the world, controlling her family, her dynasty and even European diplomacy.

One of the most perceptive writers on Queen Victoria was the historian Roger Fulford. He considered that, more than any other monarch, Victoria was 'fashioned' by the monarchy. According to him, this accounted for the contradictions in her character. 'She was stubborn but she was not inflexible. To her mother, her children and grand-children, to her courtiers and ministers she showed a side of her nature which was steely, but to circumstances and changes in her surroundings she was far less hard – indeed she changed as they changed.'[8] As well as the throne, Victoria was fashioned by her relationships with men – not only with Albert, but also with ministers such as Melbourne or Disraeli, and perhaps John Brown as well.

Victoria was indeed a woman of contradictions. I have tried not to sit in judgement on her grumpiness and selfishness. Nor have I celebrated her many different selves in postmodernist fashion, tempting though it might be to construct her as the crimson-faced and furious Queen of Hearts in Lewis Carroll's *Alice's Adventures in Wonderland*, screaming 'Off with her head!'

During the writing of this book I have been struck by the conflict (as Victoria saw it) between her role as a woman and her vocation as queen. Her relationships with her mother, her husband and her children were all distorted by this tension. Her rank did not insulate her from the pressures of an all-male political world. She considered that a female monarch was an anomaly. 'I am every day more convinced that <u>we women, if</u> we <u>are</u> to be <u>good</u> women, <u>feminine</u> and <u>amiable</u> and <u>domestic</u>, are <u>not fitted to reign</u>', she wrote in 1852.[9] But reign she must. Her strength of will in clinging to her birthright was extraordinary. Truly was it said that she had a vein of iron.[*]

From the age of thirteen Victoria wrote her journal every day of her life. She was a prolific, fluent writer, effortlessly pouring out an entry of 2,500 words or so at night before going to bed. The journal began as a semi-public document, to be read by her mother and governess, but as she grew

---

[*] Lady Lyttelton, who became governess to Victoria's children in 1840, described her thus.

older it became private and confessional. Many of the secrets that Victoria confided to her journal will never be known. From the date of her marriage to Prince Albert, the journals exist only in the version edited by Princess Beatrice, Victoria's youngest daughter, who made it her life's work to transcribe and revise her mother's diaries, destroying the originals as she went. Even the bowdlerized Princess Beatrice version is a remarkable document, however, and in 2012 the entire run – 141 volumes, comprising 43,765 pages and spanning the years 1832 to 1901 – was digitalized and made freely available online on http://www.queenvictorias journals.org/home.do Queen Victoria became immediately accessible as she had never been before.

As her journals show, Victoria was unusually self-aware. She possessed a detachment that enabled her to stand outside and reflect on her own character and on the narrative of her life. Margaret Thatcher, another powerful woman in a male-dominated political culture, never looked back, and she worked so hard that she left herself no time for self-examination.[10] Victoria, by contrast, enjoyed a remarkable ability to see the trajectory of her own story. When Albert died, she wrote: 'The poor fatherless baby of eight months is now the utterly broken-hearted and crushed widow of forty-two!'[11]

Victoria was the inventor of royal biography. After Albert's death she tried to ease her grief by composing an account of their life together. *The Early Years of the Prince Consort* appeared under the name of her private secretary, General Grey, but the book is largely compiled from the queen's own writings. Though generally ignored by scholars, it marks a milestone in the development of royal biography. It reveals with disarming frankness the private life which Prince Albert had created for the royal family.

Later, the queen commissioned Sir Theodore Martin's five-volume *Life of His Royal Highness The Prince Consort* (1875–80). Reviewers groaned as one volume after another praising the sainted Albert as a paragon among princes fell stillborn from the press. Victoria's children, however, considered that the book revealed too much about their family life. She defended her decision to publish thus: 'in these days people <u>will write</u> and <u>will</u> know, therefore the only way to counteract this, is to let the <u>real full</u> truth be <u>known</u>, and as much as <u>can be</u> with prudence and discretion, and then <u>no harm</u> but <u>good</u> will be done.'[12]

Victoria's successors however did not agree. No official biography of Queen Victoria was published after her death in 1901. Rather than commission two fat volumes of life and letters, the royal advisers led by Lord Esher took the unusual step of publishing the queen's correspondence. Three volumes of *The Letters of Queen Victoria*, taking her life up to 1861, appeared in 1907. The Edwardian editors, A. C. Benson and Esher, left out material that was judged to be sensitive or damaging. They saw nothing strange in Albert's drive for power, taking over the role of monarch and rendering Victoria incapable by making her pregnant nine times in seventeen years. The letters Victoria wrote to other women the editors thought 'very tiresome', so there is little about matters such as childbirth or clothes.[13] One effect of the Benson/Esher editorial policy was thus to redact much of the material which revealed Victoria's doubts and torment about her conflicting public and private roles.

Lytton Strachey's *Queen Victoria* (1921) is a small masterpiece – brilliantly ironic and lit by shafts of malice and wit. I have returned to it again and again, and each time I find more to admire. For Strachey, however, 'truth telling' in biography was not about exploring the private life; he was interested in exposing the gap between cant and reality, in pricking the balloons of conceit and hypocrisy. Prince Albert suffered especially from Strachey's acid pen. Albert's looks, wrote Strachey, were distressingly un-English. 'His features were regular, no doubt, but there was something smooth and smug about them; he was tall, but he was clumsily put together, and he walked with a slight slouch. Really, they thought, this youth was more like some kind of foreign tenor than anything else.' Victoria, by contrast, he described as stout, but with 'the plumpness of a vigorous matron; and an eager vitality was everywhere visible – in her energetic bearing, her protruding, enquiring glances, and her small, fat, capable and commanding hands'. Even Strachey warmed to the little, forthright queen. Few would disagree with his assessment of Victoria's fundamental characteristic: 'It was her sincerity which gave her at once her impressiveness, her charm, and her absurdity. She moved through life with the imposing certitude of one to whom concealment was impossible – either towards her surroundings or herself.'[14]

Since Elizabeth Longford published her landmark biography, attention has shifted to Victoria's family life. A great deal of material has been made available, including the important correspondence with her daughter Vicky, the Crown Princess of Germany, which escaped the censorship of the early editors (see Further Reading). Wherever possible, I have used Victoria's own writings, letting her speak in her own very distinctive voice.

Queen Victoria reigned for sixty-four years. As Strachey once remarked, 'Queen Victoria is a fine subject but she widens out alarmingly.'[15] My aim in this very small book has been to ask big questions. Why was Victoria so strong-willed as a young woman? How did her marriage change her? How did she survive the personal crisis of 1861 and how was she altered? I can only sketch the answers; space does not allow me to widen out alarmingly. But if the book has a purpose, it is to suggest that Queen Victoria's many contradictions can only be fully understood by exploring the tensions between her public role and her private life.

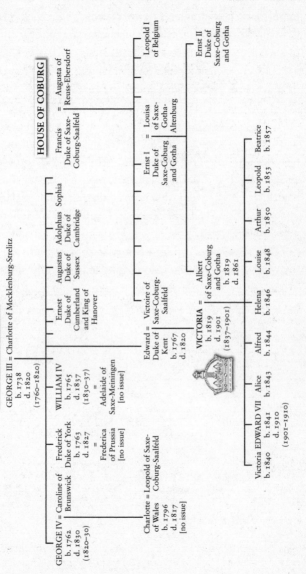

HOUSE OF HANOVER

GEORGE III = Charlotte of Mecklenburg-Strelitz
b. 1738
d. 1820
(1760–1820)

GEORGE IV = Caroline of Brunswick
b. 1762
d. 1830
(1820–30)

Frederick Duke of York
b. 1763
d. 1827
=
Frederica of Prussia
[no issue]

WILLIAM IV
b. 1765
d. 1837
(1830–37)
=
Adelaide of Saxe-Meiningen
[no issue]

Charlotte = Leopold of Saxe-Coburg-Saalfeld
b. 1796
d. 1817
[no issue]

Ernest Duke of Cumberland and King of Hanover

Augustus Duke of Sussex

Adolphus Duke of Cambridge

Sophia

Edward = Victoire of Saxe-Coburg-Saalfeld
Duke of Kent
b. 1767
d. 1820

HOUSE OF COBURG

Francis = Augusta of Reuss-Ebersdorf
Duke of Saxe-Coburg-Saalfeld

Leopold I of Belgium

Ernst I Duke of Saxe-Coburg and Gotha
=
Louisa of Saxe-Gotha-Altenburg

Ernst II Duke of Saxe-Coburg and Gotha

VICTORIA = Albert of Saxe-Coburg and Gotha
b. 1819
d. 1901
(1837–1901)
b. 1819
d. 1861

Victoria
b. 1840

EDWARD VII
b. 1841
d. 1910
(1901–1910)

Alice
b. 1843

Alfred
b. 1844

Helena
b. 1846

Louise
b. 1848

Arthur
b. 1850

Leopold
b. 1853

Beatrice
b. 1857

Victoria

I

'A Resolute Little Tit'

Kensington Palace, London, 20 June 1837. At 6 a.m. the eighteen-year-old Princess Victoria is woken by her mother, in whose bedroom she sleeps, and told that the Archbishop of Canterbury and Lord Chamberlain wish to see her. She goes to them (as she writes in her diary) '<u>alone</u>'. They tell her that her uncle, King William IV, has died in the night, and 'consequently that I am <u>Queen</u>'. At 9 she sees the prime minister Lord Melbourne in her room, 'and of <u>course quite alone</u> as I shall <u>always</u> do all my Ministers'. At 11.30, wearing a black silk dress, she walks downstairs and holds a Privy Council – her Accession Council – 'of course quite alone'.[1]

The young queen, with her precocious self-possession and fresh-skinned innocence, touched the hearts of the crusty political grandees assembled in the council at Kensington Palace. For an eighteen-year-old it was a performance of astonishing bravura, but she behaved in a way that we might consider tough and ruthless. When she wrote 'alone', she meant without her mother, the Duchess of Kent. Still a teenager, she broke off relations with her mother and refused to speak to her, even though the duchess had until a few weeks previously expected to become regent. As the diarist Thomas Creevey observed, the new queen was 'a resolute little tit'.[2]

3

What was the source of Victoria's steeliness?

Queen Victoria owed her very existence to the dynastic crisis that engulfed the Hanoverian monarchy after 1817. She was the daughter of the fourth son of George III, Prince Edward Duke of Kent. George III had seven sons, but though they fathered over twenty illegitimate children between them, there was only one legitimate child: Princess Charlotte, the daughter of George IV. When the twenty-one-year-old Charlotte died in childbirth in 1817, the Hanoverians faced extinction. As Shelley railed in 'England in 1819': 'An old, mad, blind despised, and dying King/ Princes, the dregs of their dull race . . .'.

The men whom Victoria later called her wicked uncles – middle-aged roués, living in sin with their mistresses – were forced to set about begetting an heir. The Prince Regent (soon to become George IV) was locked into a broken marriage to Caroline of Brunswick, and the Duke of York (brother number two) was married without children. This created an opening for four younger sons – the Duke of Clarence (number three), later King William IV, the Duke of Kent (number four), the Duke of Cumberland (number five) and the Duke of Cambridge (number seven).*

Victoria was the result of an arranged marriage between the Duke of Kent and a German princess. In 1817 the duke

---

* The sixth brother, the Duke of Sussex, had ruled himself out of the race by marrying Lady Augusta Murray in contravention of the Royal Marriages Act (1772), which ordained that no descendant of George II could marry without the consent of the reigning monarch.

was fifty – tall and bald with dyed brown whiskers. Victoria liked to boast that she was a soldier's daughter, but her father could not be said to have been successful in that career. He served through the Revolutionary and Napoleonic wars, but he only saw action once, in the West Indies. Most of the time he was safely away from the fighting in British North America (today Canada). He was a liability because of his brutality towards his men. On the parade ground he was a fiend. Posted to Gibraltar in 1802, his attempts to restore discipline in the drunken garrison provoked a near-mutiny, and he was ordered to leave.[3] In private life, however, the stubborn martinet was a decent man. He lived openly with his mistress, Madame de Saint-Laurent, but the relationship was domestic and uxorious. His chief failing was his debts, which were a public scandal. In the crisis created by Charlotte's death, the Duke of Kent did not hesitate to do his duty. He ditched his mistress of twenty-seven years and married Victoire of Saxe-Coburg, the thirty-year-old widow of a minor German ruler, the Prince of Leiningen.

The dynastic calculation behind this marriage is crucially important. Victoire was the sister of Prince Leopold of Saxe-Coburg, who was the husband of Princess Charlotte. It was Leopold who persuaded his sister to give up her independence as regent of the tiny German state of Amorbach and marry the Duke of Kent in a bid for the British throne. Leopold was a handsome, ambitious adventurer, the younger son of the Duke of Coburg. Cheated in his personal bid for the British throne by Charlotte's death, he engineered a second line of attack by marrying his sister to

Charlotte's uncle. Thanks to the madness of George III and his dysfunctional children, the Hanoverians were a dynasty in meltdown, ripe for takeover.

When Victoire became pregnant, the Duke of Kent determined to stamp his child's claim to the British crown. The Kents were living in Amorbach, deep in the middle of Germany, and the duke insisted that the baby should be born in England. Short of money as ever, he drove the coach himself, sitting on the box as it trundled along rutted roads for 430 miles with his heavily pregnant wife bumping about inside. Victoria was born at Kensington Palace on 24 May 1819, and the birth was witnessed by the Archbishop of Canterbury and the political grandees whose presence was then considered necessary for a child in direct line of succession.

The Duke of Kent's pushiness about his daughter's claims irritated his spoilt and tricky older brother, the Prince Regent. He revenged himself by ruining the christening. The name Victoria seems to us indelibly printed on the age, but it came about as the result of a spat. The Kents had chosen a string of royal names – Georgiana, Charlotte, Augusta. These were all vetoed by the Regent; Charlotte, the name of his dead daughter, he considered too presumptuous and Augusta too majestic, while he would not allow the child to be baptized Georgiana after him. On the day of the christening in Buckingham Palace, the archbishop stood holding the baby at the font, and waited for the Regent to pronounce. He declared that she should be baptized Alexandrina, after Tsar Alexander I, her sponsor, and Victoria, an anglicized version of her mother's name.[4] This foreign-sounding invented name was intended to distance the child from the British throne. Later, William IV thought it so unsuitable for a British queen that he tried to persuade Victoria to change it. Victoria was a name, he grumbled, 'which is not English, had never been known heretofore as a Christian name in this country, not even German but of French origin'.[5] The princess, who was then twelve, refused, and so did her mother. When she became queen she insisted on being proclaimed Victoria and dropped the Alexandrina.

The Duke of Kent died suddenly of pneumonia when Victoria was only eight months old. Victoire found herself a widow once more – she 'kills all her husbands', remarked Princess Lieven, the formidable wife of the Russian ambassador.[6] Six days later, on 29 January 1820, King George III died and the Regent succeeded as George IV. At this point Leopold made one more crucial intervention. Victoire had no money, having inherited nothing but debts from her husband. But rather than allow her to return to Amorbach with her baby, as she desired and George IV wished, Leopold paid for her to remain in London, giving her an allowance which enabled her (just) to live at Kensington Palace.

It was thus thanks to Leopold that Victoria was brought up in England by her mother. The duchess was 'tall and big, very pale with black eyes and black hair'.[7] (Why the child of two tall parents grew up to be so short is a mystery.) Victoire was gorgeously dressed in silks and bright velvets, and some portraits show a swarthy face. Princess Lieven thought her 'the most mediocre person it would be possible to meet'.[8] She never mastered the English language, but she insisted that her daughter – who was three-quarters German – learned English not German as her first language. 'Never spoke German until 1839,' wrote Victoria. 'Not allowed to.'[9]

As a small child at Kensington Palace, Victoria was spoilt, as she herself admitted.[10] She was effectively an only child – her half-sister Feodore was twelve years older – adored by a doting single parent. Her mother showered her with cloyingly affectionate notes, written in broken English on pink paper. And the little girl who resembled George III in petticoats was addressed as Your Royal Highness, followed wherever she went by a scarlet-liveried footman, waited upon and knelt before. When a visiting child tried to play with her toys, the six-year-old princess remarked: 'You must not touch those, they are mine; and I may call you Jane, but you must not call me Victoria.'[11] In adult life, Victoria sometimes displayed a wilfulness, stubbornness and lack of empathy which reminded perceptive observers of a spoilt child.

From about the age of eleven, however, her regime at Kensington changed. Victoria told her daughter Vicky in 1858:

I had a very unhappy life as a child – had no scope for my very violent feelings of affection – had no brothers or sisters to live with – never had a father – from my unfortunate circumstances was not on comfortable or at all intimate or confidential footing with my mother ... and did not know what a happy domestic life was![12]

Ramsgate, October–November 1835. Victoria, now sixteen, has come here for a holiday and fallen dangerously ill. For five weeks she is confined to her room with a high fever. She is devotedly nursed by her governess, the Hanoverian Baroness Lehzen. Her mother, however, crossly dismisses her symptoms as exaggerated, and refuses to call a doctor. Only when Victoria becomes delirious does the reluctant duchess agree to send for the royal physician, Dr James Clark. He diagnoses typhoid.

While she is still very weak, her mother's friend and factotum Sir John Conroy comes to her room. A dishonest, handsome rogue, Conroy has been busily spreading rumours that Victoria is backward and incapable. Abetted by the duchess, he presents her with a document to sign, pledging to appoint him her private secretary when she becomes queen. As Victoria later told Lord Melbourne: 'I resisted in spite of my illness, and their harshness – my beloved Lehzen supporting me alone.'[13]

This was a life-changing experience. Victoria never forgot how ill she had been at Ramsgate. Nor did she forgive her mother for her hard-hearted lack of sympathy. Worse still, she came to see that Conroy and her mother were in league and plotting to rob her of her power.

For the past five years or so Conroy and the duchess had subjected Victoria to a controlling regime which Conroy later dubbed the Kensington system. After the death of her uncle George IV in 1830, Victoria stood next in line to the throne, and she was generally accepted as heiress presumptive.* Her uncle William IV was an asthmatic sixty-four-year-old, and it seemed probable that she would succeed before she reached eighteen, the moment when royal persons came of age. The purpose of the Kensington system was to ensure that the Duchess of Kent became regent – with Conroy at her elbow – if Victoria inherited as a minor. To this end, 'every effort must be made to keep the education of the daughter completely in the hands of her mother ... *nothing* and *no one* should be able to tear the daughter away from her.'[14] Victoria was cut off from the court of William IV, who loathed the duchess, and wished to remove Victoria from her care.

From 1832, the duchess embarked on a programme of semi-royal progresses, dragging the teenage Victoria round the great Whig houses (William IV was a Tory, so the duchess identified with his opponents) and showing her to the people. Victoria detested these tours and complained of feeling ill. The training was remorseless. At Plymouth in 1833 she was required to jump from a ship, and though she meekly did as she was told, close observers noticed that she was weeping with fright. At a luncheon, she could be seen looking intently first at one person and then another. She

---

* Under the law of succession as it stood until 2013, a female heir to the throne could never be heir apparent, as the birth of a son to the monarch would defeat her claim, and he would become heir apparent. William IV was still hopeful of producing an heir, but none of Queen Adelaide's babies lived.

was learning her lesson, said Conroy: afterwards the duchess would question her about all the guests. The names can be seen carefully listed in her journal.

Conroy was an ambitious schemer and a charlatan. He embezzled money from Victoria's aunt, the blind Princess Sophia, and, acting as the Duchess of Kent's comptroller, he defrauded her of large sums over many years.[16] Whether Conroy was the dictator at Kensington Palace, however, is debatable. In later years, it suited the family to believe that the duchess was an innocent victim who had been manipulated by Conroy. They blamed King Leopold for failing to intervene. 'Mama here would never have fallen into the hands of Conroy, if Uncle Leopold had taken the trouble to guide her,' wrote Albert.[17] In the 1907 edition of the *Letters of Queen Victoria*, the harsh treatment and bullying that Victoria endured at Kensington Palace in the years before her accession was suppressed.

The duchess was a tough survivor, battle-hardened by the Borgia-like plotting of small German courts. The Kensington system was not forced upon her. At the very least she was complicit, and it seems far more likely that she was Conroy's accomplice than his puppet. He was rumoured (probably wrongly) to be her lover, though some said that Victoria had witnessed 'familiarities' between them. And it was true that the duchess had form in this regard. In her days as a young widow at Amorbach, she had enjoyed an intimate relationship with her Master of the Horse, a James Hewitt-type officer named Captain Schindler, whom she promoted Master of the Household, allowing him to share her powers as regent.

The Kensington system meant that Victoria grew up with her mother as her jailer. In adolescence, when parental control might have been relaxed, it was tightened. Victoria slept every night in a bed in her mother's room. She was not allowed to walk downstairs without holding someone's hand. She was kept in isolation and under constant surveillance, and she was forbidden to meet anyone without a third party being present. Though treated as a prisoner, she was like a spoilt child in one important sense – she was never allowed to be on equal terms with friends of her own age.

Her closest friend was her much older half-sister, Feodore Leiningen. The duchess worried that Feodore was a bad influence, and when Victoria was eight Feodore was banished – married off to an impoverished German prince. This was harsh, for (as Victoria later wrote) one of the penalties of being royal was that 'we <u>cannot form</u> intimate friendships <u>except</u> among our <u>nearest relations</u>'.[18] By nature an extrovert, she made her dolls act as substitutes for friends. Rather than pretend they were babies, the princess dressed her collection of 132 small dolls (all but two were female) as adults, wearing the costumes of characters from plays and operas. Throughout her life Victoria dreaded being alone; but childhood loneliness perhaps taught her how to cope with solitude.

The Kensington system had some strengths. For one thing, Victoria received a reasonable education. To prove her fitness for bringing up her daughter, the duchess needed to demonstrate that she was providing an appropriate education for the heir to the throne. Aged eleven, Victoria was formally examined by two bishops who – predictably perhaps – gave her a glowing report. Her curriculum was designed to teach the necessary accomplishments without compromising female decorum. By the standards of aristocratic girls she was well schooled. She spoke and wrote French fluently, she spoke good German and she learned some Latin, though no Greek. But the rooms at Kensington Palace were not lined with books to stimulate her intellectual curiosity. Nor did the duchess's dull and inward-looking court sharpen Victoria's wits with the cut and thrust of clever *salon* talk. As Lord Melbourne later remarked: 'The rest of her education she owes to her own natural shrewdness and quickness, and this perhaps has not been a proper education for one who was to wear the Crown of England.'[19]

When Victoria was eleven, her mother judged the moment right to tell her she would be queen. 'I will be good', she is reported (probably apocryphally) to have vowed.[20] More to the point, knowledge of her vocation made the regime at Kensington bearable, and gave her a strong sense of self-worth. In retrospect, it was no bad thing that Victoria was distanced from the court of William IV, and so untarnished by the dissolute gerontocracy of her Hanoverian uncles.

The threats at Kensington were considerable, however. Victoria was bullied by Conroy and her mother. They taunted her with being ugly and stupid – too childish to reign, even when she reached the age of eighteen. Today we would call this emotional abuse. (There is no suggestion that Conroy abused Victoria physically, though her horror and hatred of him does make one wonder.) As Feodore wrote in 1836, 'she has suffered a good deal' and 'her car-acter [*sic*] might be completely spoiled by this continual warfare'.[21] Feodore was perceptive: Victoria was indeed scarred.

Victoria's eighteenth birthday on 24 May 1837 triggered rows that were more furious and hysterical than ever. Not only were Conroy and the duchess cheated of their hopes of a regency: when King William offered Victoria an establishment of her own, they became frantic. Enraged at this attempt to break her control over her daughter, the duchess unwisely refused the king's offer without consulting Victoria. As King William lay on his deathbed, Conroy demanded once more that Victoria appoint him her private secretary and threatened to coerce her. At length her uncle Leopold, who since 1831 had been King of the Belgians, intervened, though far too late to stop the damage. He sent Baron Stockmar, the physician who acted as his political adviser, to London.

If the Kensington system threatened Victoria, however, it also taught her how to survive. Stockmar was impressed by her toughness. He found her 'extremely jealous of what she considers to be her rights and her future power'.[22] It was at Kensington that Victoria developed the 'vein of iron' that was central to her character. And it was this steeli-ness that enabled her to break the stranglehold of her mother and Conroy. Paradoxically, the Kensington system made Victoria so strong that she was able to defeat its entire object. She dumped her mother, banished Conroy and ruled 'alone'.

2
Camelot

Victoria came to the throne amidst immense popularity and goodwill. Her youth and purity seemed to promise a new dawn. Her coronation, on 27 June 1838, was attended by the biggest crowds ever known in London, brought into the city by the new railroads. 'Their good-humour and excessive loyalty was beyond everything,' she wrote, 'and I really cannot say <u>how</u> proud I feel to be the Queen of <u>such</u> a <u>Nation</u>.'[1] A few months later, Victoria blundered into one of the worst crises of her reign – a toxic mix of smear stories and unconstitutional behaviour. Her popularity evaporated. How did this come about, and to what extent was Victoria herself to blame?

'I cannot resist telling you,' wrote Creevey, 'that our dear little Queen in every respect is *perfection*.'[2] The princess whom the diarist Charles Greville had described at the age of twelve in 1831 as 'a short, vulgar looking child', had grown up. She was still short, no more than 4 feet 11 inches, and often in her diary she bewailed her failure to grow. Her fair hair had darkened, but she was proud of its abundance. She had very blue eyes and excellent skin, and people praised her demeanour or posture. She had a tendency to keep her mouth open – her sister Feodore begged her to close it when her portrait was being done, but most artists paint the young Victoria with parted lips and large teeth. She laughed (Creevey again) 'in real earnest, opening her mouth as wide as it will go, showing not very pretty gums', and she gobbled her food, but she 'blushes and laughs every instant in so natural a way as to disarm anybody'.[3] She was attractively unselfconscious about her looks, utterly lacking in personal vanity and always ready to admire handsomeness in others. She had a naturally beautiful voice.

Victoria was the youngest person to come to the throne since the Tudor boy king Edward VI, who had been ten, even younger than her grandfather George III, who had been twenty-two. She had received barely any preparation for becoming queen. The only person who had attempted to instruct her was Leopold. He wrote often around the time of her accession, counselling her to remain cool and never to allow herself to be forced into making an instant decision.[4] She knew very little about the monarch's political position.

Her first act was to break with her mother, and deny her access to her apartments. 'I had to remind her <u>who</u> I was.' She refused to allow the duchess to take the title and precedence of Queen Mother.[5] The adolescent child of an abusive parent, she now found herself with absolute power over her mother, and she did not scruple to revenge herself. Shortly after the accession she moved into Buckingham Palace. The duchess was banished to a distant part of the palace and ordered to send a note if she wished to see her daughter; and Victoria was usually too busy. Baroness Lehzen, by contrast, was rewarded for her loyalty with a bedroom joined by a communicating door to that of the queen.

Victoria bonded at once with her prime minister, Lord Melbourne. The fifty-eight-year-old widower was still strikingly handsome, and the young queen was captivated by his worldly Whig cynicism. Her journal records seeing 'Lord M' for an hour or so each day, and he often dined in the evening too; he had an office at Buckingham Palace and a room at Windsor. Melbourne told her about her Hanoverian family, of which she knew very little, he chattered about British politics and history, and he gossiped about the aristocracy, a subject on which Victoria was to remain remarkably well informed throughout her life. In her journal, which escaped Princess Beatrice's pruning for these years, Victoria carefully transcribed his conversation. More than anyone, Melbourne deserves credit for teaching Victoria how to be queen – and for making her a British queen rather than a German one.

At Windsor, where the court moved in August, Victoria took long rides – she was an intrepid horsewoman, and she often galloped for two hours at a time. 'Lord Melbourne rode near me the whole time,' she wrote; 1837 was 'the pleasantest summer <u>I</u> <u>ever</u> passed in <u>my life</u>'.[6] Under the guidance of Melbourne, constantly at the queen's side, the court became 'a stainless Camelot' of high ideals.[7]

Before her accession, Victoria later confessed, she '<u>never</u> could ... take the slightest interest in Public affairs'.[8] As a teenager, this was hardly strange; but what was extraordinary was the expectation that at eighteen – an age which made her a minor for all purposes except succeeding to the throne – she should be able to do the work of the crown unaided. When she became queen, Victoria asked Sir Herbert Taylor, who had acted as unofficial private secretary to her blind, mad grandfather George III, whether she should have a private secretary. 'Is Your Majesty afraid of the work?' he replied. She said she wasn't, and Taylor told her that she should not have a private secretary.

The private secretary's office originated, as one historian has written, 'not in the sovereign's readiness for business, but in the sovereign's incapacity for business'.[9] For Victoria to appoint a secretary would be to signal her own incapacity. Moreover, the office was viewed with suspicion, as a malign and mischievous influence, poisoning the sovereign against her ministers. This was the job to which the scoundrel Conroy had aspired. King Leopold also had his eye on it for his envoy Stockmar. Rather than appoint someone who might plot against him, Melbourne did the work of private secretary himself. He drafted business letters for the queen, read aloud political correspondence to her and advised on appointments.

Melbourne has been criticized for failing to teach the queen compassion for the other nation – the poor.* More immediately, by combining the private secretary's work with the premiership, Melbourne created a conflict of interest for himself. He encouraged Victoria to think that he was *her* minister. She failed to grasp the change in the position of the monarch that had come about as a consequence of

---

* The awakening of Victoria's social conscience and her disillusion with Melbourne's lack of compassion is the theme of the film *The Young Victoria*.

the 1832 Reform Act, which meant that governments were appointed by Parliament, not the queen.

The scandal that erupted over Lady Flora Hastings less than two years after Victoria's accession did not blow up out of a clear blue sky. It was intimately linked to the Kensington system. The feud between Victoria and her mother meant that two rival courts coexisted under the same roof at Buckingham Palace. One of Victoria's first acts had been to pension off Conroy and give him a baronetcy, but he still lurked in the duchess's apartments. Victoria refused to receive him, but he seemed impossible to get rid of. Lady Flora Hastings was another hated figure from the Kensington era who reappeared as lady-in-waiting to the duchess. A sharp-tongued spinster in her early thirties from a Tory family, she was believed by Victoria to be a spy.

In February 1839, Victoria told Lord Melbourne that she had noticed a change in Lady Flora's figure, and that she was 'to use the plain words – <u>with child</u>!' The father, Victoria was convinced, was the 'Monster and Demon Incarnate', Conroy.[10] When, over sixty years later, King Edward VII read the letters about this episode, he was 'astonished at the precocious knowledge shown by the Queen and the outspokenness of Lord Melbourne'.[11]

Soon the court seethed with gossip about the pregnancy. Eventually, in order to clear her name, Lady Flora submitted to a full medical examination. The doctors found her to be a virgin, though her abdomen and perhaps her womb was enlarged. The queen apologized to her. Lady Flora, meanwhile, informed her family, and her brother, the Marquess of Hastings, wrote to Melbourne complaining about the way the matter had been handled. When the Hastings family received no satisfaction, they published letters in the newspapers. Conroy busily stirred the scandal, inciting the Duchess of Kent, who exploited Lady Flora's case to expose her daughter's heartless treatment of *her*. It worked. The newspapers filled with stories about the sufferings of Lady Flora, and the cruel, immoral conduct of the court. Victoria's Camelot was revealed as a harem seething with spitefulness and sexual intrigue.

This squalid scandal was the background to the 'Bedchamber Crisis'. Melbourne's resignation when his government lost its majority in May 1839 made the queen hysterical with grief. As her journals show, she had become utterly dependent on Lord Melbourne emotionally, confiding in him her hatred of her mother and counting on his support in the rift. Melbourne, for his part, was dangerously besotted with his little queen.

Robert Peel, attempting to form a Tory minority government, asked the queen for an assurance of her support by dismissing the Whig ladies of her bedchamber. Constitutional practice was unclear on this point: incoming ministers normally appointed new gentlemen at court, not ladies, but Peel argued that a female sovereign changed matters. Peel's demand was politically savvy, as it highlighted the treatment of the Tory Flora Hastings. Defying constitutional convention, Victoria asked for advice from Melbourne, the outgoing prime minister. With Melbourne's support, she refused Peel's request to change her ladies.

Victoria got her way. Peel declined to form a government, and Melbourne and the Whigs returned to office. This was the last time a monarch blocked the formation of a government to which she was politically opposed. Greville considered it 'a high trial of our institutions when the caprice of a girl of nineteen can overturn a great ministerial combination'.[12] Victoria herself later blamed Melbourne for making her 'a party Queen'. But by being partisan Victoria was only acting as her predecessors had done: William IV had been just as partisan a Tory as she was a Whig.[13] Melbourne should have known better than to agree to her request for advice. But by acting as her private secretary, Melbourne ensured that when he resigned as prime minister the queen had no one to turn to.

At Buckingham Palace, Lady Flora lay gravely ill (why her family allowed her to die in this way is a puzzle). Victoria complained to Melbourne that it was 'disagreeable' to have a dying person in her palace. She visited Lady Flora a few days before her death and observed that, though as thin as a skeleton, her body was 'very much swollen like a person who is with child'.[14] When Lady Flora died, probably of liver cancer, Victoria showed no compassion, telling Melbourne that she felt '<u>no</u> remorse, I felt <u>I</u> had done nothing to kill her'.[15] Two Tory ladies hissed her as she drove up the course at Ascot races, and Victoria told Melbourne that she wished she could have them flogged.*[16]

The little Whig queen, who only a year ago had been the

---

* It is still not clear what really happened in the Flora Hastings affair. Many of the papers at Windsor concerning the case were destroyed on the orders of Edward VII. It is probably significant that Conroy abruptly left the duchess's service a few weeks before Flora Hastings' death.

nation's darling, was now (according to Greville) as unpopular as her uncle George IV had been at the time of his divorce from Queen Caroline.[17] She put on weight, which was always a bad sign with her – eating was her reaction to stress.* She complained that she was disgusted and tired with everything. As Stockmar observed, Victoria was 'as passionate as a spoilt child, if she feels offended she throws everything overboard without exception'.[18] Where could she go from here?

* In December 1838 she weighed 8 stone 13 pounds, 'an incredible weight for my size' (Cecil Woodham-Smith, *Queen Victoria*, p. 163). This gives a BMI of 25.2, which places her at the lower end of the overweight spectrum according to modern measurements, but by no means obese.

3
Albert

Coburg, 29–30 August 1824. Albert, aged five, who is alert but small for his age, with curly fair hair, has driven with his brother Ernest and his father, Duke Ernest (who is the brother of the Duchess of Kent) to the Schloss Ehrenburg, the ducal palace in the centre of the town. Coburg is in uproar. Angry crowds throng the streets and force an entrance into the palace, pushing past the duke, who jostles with one of the leaders. Fortunately, the family apartments in the palace, which has been recently rebuilt, are high up on the second floor. Albert's mother, the twenty-three-year-old Duchess Louise, has been forced to agree to a separation from her husband and abandon her children, supposedly because she has committed adultery. But the Coburgers worship her, partly because she spends her money on helping the poor. When Louise left the city a couple of days earlier, the crowd removed the horses from her carriage and pulled her back, cheering wildly.

Duke Ernest, who suspects – wrongly – that Louise has inspired the revolt, is angry. He is also frightened. This is the first rebellion that Coburg has known, and his throne is in danger. So too are his family's ambitious plans for the marriage of his small son Albert to the future Queen of

England. He wants to order the militia to fire on the crowd, but he is restrained.

After three days of riots, the turmoil subsides. Ernest savagely punishes the ringleaders. At midnight on 4 September, Louise leaves Coburg for ever. 'Parting from the children was the worst thing of all,' she wrote. 'They have whooping cough, and they said, "Mama is crying because she has to go away when we are ill".'[1]

Visiting the sleepy city of Coburg, deep in the landlocked Thuringian plain, reached by means of a lengthy journey on small trains with an un-Teutonic tendency to be late, I was struck by the contrast between Prince Albert's towering ambition and his provincial small-town origins. Coburg today is a city of 42,000 people, about the size of Winchester or Salisbury. Then, with a population of 9,000, it was the capital of a Saxon duchy of 200 square miles, half the size of the Isle of Wight. The Saxe-Coburgs, whose family name was Wettin, were princes of the Holy Roman Empire and could trace their ancestry back to the dukes of Saxony in the eleventh century. In the new era of the nation-state these petty princes were beginning to seem redundant, yet, paradoxically, this was the moment when the Wettin dynasty rocketed to greatness, placing its offspring on the thrones of Belgium, Portugal and, most importantly, Britain.[2] As the riots of 1824 vividly illustrated, however, Coburg was a fragile launch pad for their ambitions.

Louise, the wronged duchess adored by the mob, was the spoilt, liberal-minded heiress to the neighbouring duchy of

Gotha-Altenburg, a state twice the size of Coburg.* Aged sixteen she made an arranged marriage to the thirty-two-year-old Duke Ernest. Intelligent and lively, Louise expected to find in Ernest a chivalric knight after the fashion of Walter Scott – a dream which Ernest encouraged by decorating the Rosenau, their miniature castle outside Coburg, in the latest gothic style. How mortifying to discover that Ernest was a tight-fisted boor, who spent his time hunting animals and chasing other women. Louise retaliated by engaging in very public flirtations with members of her household.

Ernest accused Louise of being unfaithful, and some have speculated that Albert was the son of a Jewish court chamberlain. These were smear stories, invented by Ernest's party to justify the divorce.†[3] It seems more likely that the marriage of Ernest and Louise was blown apart by a public scandal. In 1823 there was published in Paris a scurrilous memoir or *libelle* by an ex-mistress of Ernest's named Pauline Panam, who accused Ernest of having an affair with her

---

* Her father, Duke Augustus of Saxe-Gotha-Altenburg, was cultured, enjoyed wearing women's clothes and was probably gay – he wrote one of the first novels to celebrate same-sex love.

† A modern story holds that Albert's real father was his uncle Leopold, who visited Coburg shortly after the death of his wife, Princess Charlotte. Although the dates match, this is no more than speculation. There is no mention of Leopold's name in contemporary accounts, nor is there evidence of any rift in Leopold's relations with his brother Ernest.

as a fourteen-year-old and alleged that he was the father of her son. These claims were wildly exaggerated, but Ernest, who was blackmailed by Panam, seems to have believed that Louise was in league with her.[4]

Ernest's domineering mother, old Duchess Augusta, now intervened. A beaky-nosed matriarch of iron will, she was remembered by her grandchild Victoria as 'a most remarkable woman, with a most powerful, energetic, almost masculine mind'.[5] Victoria's use of the word masculine is revealing. It was Duchess Augusta who had saved the Saxe-Coburgs from extinction when Napoleon's armies invaded by sending her sons to Paris to plead for the restoration of ducal rule in 1807. By making strategic marriages for her nine children she was the architect of Coburg's dizzying rise. She had engineered the marriage of Ernest to Louise, who brought much-needed Gotha cash into the impoverished Coburg treasury. But when Louise became a liability, Duchess Augusta did not hesitate to urge Ernest to divorce.

Louise was a wronged, defenceless and rather foolish young woman, no match for Duchess Augusta and her son. She was banished to the distant town of Wendel, 300 miles from Coburg. Here she married an officer named Von Hanstein, who was sent by Duke Ernest to take care of her. Louise never saw her children again. She signed away all her money to Ernest, and in 1826, after the death of her uncle, he added Gotha to his lands and the name of the duchy changed to Saxe-Coburg-Gotha.

Louise died aged thirty-one of cancer of the uterus – or possibly the cervix – the victim of the ruthless ambition (and perhaps the sexually transmitted diseases) of the

Saxe-Coburg dynasty. Duke Ernest married his niece Marie of Württemberg, the daughter of his sister Antoinette, an alliance that would have been prohibited under the tables of affinity in the Church of England's *Book of Common Prayer*. It is perhaps little wonder that this poor woman's expression was so sour that even the Coburg court painters were unable to make her portrait remotely sympathetic. The marriage was childless, but it meant that Albert's first cousin was also his stepmother, a relationship that was incestuous by English standards.

Albert looked very like his mother and inherited her lively mind, and she openly acknowledged him as her favourite. His biographer dismissed Louise's love for her son as 'a distracting influence', but her disappearance was a deeply traumatic event in Albert's childhood.[6] As a small boy, he was sickly and often in tears, which he pathetically recorded in his diary.

When Albert was not yet four he and Ernest were put in the charge of a tutor named Christopher Florschutz, who stayed for fifteen years. A needy, brainy child, Albert learned to escape from his sorrows by working, and he thrived on the intensive princely education he received from Florschutz in the Rosenau. He was surrounded entirely by men; from a very early age, Albert 'showed a great dislike to being in the charge of women'.[7]

Marriage between the two first cousins Albert and Victoria had been projected by their scheming grandmother Duchess Augusta ever since they were delivered by the same midwife.[8] When Albert was sixteen he and his brother visited Kensington Palace. Victoria thought Albert 'very stout'; he disliked court life, fell asleep in the evenings and suffered a bilious attack.[9] Disappointed by his protégé's poor performance, Uncle Leopold took charge, appointing his adviser Baron Stockmar to groom Albert for the role of ruler. A year at the university of Bonn followed by a tour of Italy transformed the fat teenager into a polished and studious prince who looked older than his age. He still yawned after dinner, but Stockmar somehow instilled into the motherless boy an astonishing sense of self-worth and entitlement. Aged nineteen, the prince told his uncle Leopold that if Victoria kept him waiting for more than three years 'it would ruin all the prospects of my future life'.[10]

Windsor Castle, 10 October 1839, 7.30 p.m. Victoria stands at the top of the grand staircase to receive Albert and his brother Ernest, who have arrived from their sea crossing without their luggage. 'It was with some emotion that I beheld Albert – who is <u>beautiful</u>,' wrote Victoria. Before the visit Victoria has made it clear that she has no intention of marrying; but she finds Albert so 'excessively handsome' that 'My heart is quite <u>going</u>.' On the second day, she sends Albert a message saying that 'he had made a very favourable impression on her'. On the 13th she tells Lord Melbourne that seeing the brothers 'had a good deal changed my opinion (as to marrying) and that I must decide soon'. The following day she informs Melbourne that she has made up her mind 'about marrying dearest Albert, whom I <u>adore</u>'. Nor is she in any doubt as to who should propose. 'I asked if I hadn't better tell Albert of my [*sic*] decision soon, in which Lord M. agreed; how? I asked, for that in general such things were done the other way, – which made Lord M. and me laugh very much.' She sends Albert another message, warning him that she will probably make a declaration to him shortly.[11]

The following morning at 12.30 she asks Albert to come alone to her closet. They sit together in the little blue room on the little blue sofa.

> I said to him that I thought he must be aware <u>why</u> I wished them to come here, – and that it would make me <u>too happy</u> if he would consent to what I wished (to marry me); we embraced each other over and over again, and he was <u>so</u> kind, <u>so</u> affectionate; oh! to <u>feel</u> I was, and am, loved by <u>such</u> an Angel as Albert was <u>too great delight</u> to describe! he is <u>perfection</u>; perfection in every way, – in beauty – in everything![12]

As sovereign, Victoria needed to ask no one's permission. The only person she told beforehand was Melbourne.* Her mother was not informed. For a woman to propose to a man was unprecedented – a century later, Queen Elizabeth II was proposed to by Prince Philip (though it's true that

---

* The comparison with Edward VIII is instructive. The Royal Marriages Act does not apply to the sovereign. But Edward VIII's proposed marriage to Wallis Simpson was blocked by Baldwin, implying the Cabinet's right to consent to the marriage. Victoria, by contrast, merely informed Melbourne of her decision to marry Albert; she did not feel obliged to seek her ministers' consent, and nor did they consider that it was in their power to control her choice of consort.

in 1946 she was a princess and not yet a queen).[13] Victoria made up her mind astonishingly quickly, after only a few hours, and proposed five days later. As her diary makes plain, it was a *coup de foudre*; Albert's beauty infatuated her.

As for Albert, he had come to Windsor resolved to break off relations with his cousin, disgusted by reports of her stubbornness and late-night partying.[14] The suddenness of Victoria's proposal came as a shock. That evening he retired early with a nosebleed. But he was triumphant. Marriage to Victoria was Albert's career, the job for which he had spent his life preparing. The couple enjoyed a 'heavenly' month together at Windsor, and during that time they always spoke German. The language that Victoria had been forbidden to speak as a child at Kensington Palace was now for her the language of love.[15]

They were married on 10 February 1840 at the Chapel Royal, St James's. Albert wore the uniform of a British Field Marshal and the Order of the Garter. Florence Nightingale commented that he was so poor he had to borrow clothes to be married in.[16]

4
The Taming of the Shrew

The marriage of Victoria and Albert has been represented – not least by Victoria herself – as one of the great love stories of all time. That Victoria was besotted is abundantly clear. Winterhalter's 'secret' bedroom portrait of her aged twenty-four with her head thrown back, loosened hair falling over her bare shoulder and parted lips, wearing a dress which resembles a nightgown, is as explicit as a court painting could be about her feelings for Albert.[1] But the marriage was also a battleground and a struggle for mastery. Albert, the romantic lover who, on the morning after the marriage, 'looked more beautiful than it is possible for me to say' in his black velvet jacket and Byronic open white shirt without a neckcloth, was also a calculating, controlling careerist who had been trained for rule.[2] By convincing Victoria that she was morally flawed and unwomanly, he persuaded her to surrender power. Victoria, the fatherless child, who as a thirteen-year-old had found an allegory of female submission in *The Taming of the Shrew*, was ready to comply.[3]

In the first months after her marriage, Victoria did all she could to advance Albert's status. As a Prince of

Coburg, Albert was a mere Serene Highness – the lowest grade of German royalty. Victoria promoted him to the highest rank, creating him a Royal Highness days before the wedding.[4] Enraged by the cuts that Parliament made to his allowance, she fought to grant him precedence over her Hanoverian relations, and she blushed with pleasure when Parliament agreed to appoint him regent in the event of her death.

Precedence, however, was one thing; power was quite another. Victoria allowed Albert to blot the ink on her letters, but she preferred it when he undid her stockings. When Albert suggested a honeymoon, Victoria snapped: 'You forget, my dearest Love, that I am the Sovereign, and that business can stop and wait for nothing.' Albert complained, 'I am only the husband and not the master in the house'.*[5]

Victoria – to her fury – found herself pregnant within weeks of the marriage, and Albert seized his chance. He moved his writing table into her room at Windsor and placed it next to hers. There was a similar arrangement at Buckingham Palace, where the two identical tables stood side by side (on Albert's side the drawers were shallower to allow for his higher chair). 'I have come to be extremely pleased with Victoria during the past few months,' wrote

---

* The royal children did not take Albert's surname. Though he didn't complain, Albert was in this respect like Prince Philip, who described himself as 'a bloody amoeba', the only man in the country not allowed to give his name to his children. Victoria and Albert's children were registered under the Hanoverian name of Guelph.

Albert. 'She has only twice had the sulks . . . altogether she puts more confidence in me daily.'[6] In November 1840, when her first child was born, Victoria gave Albert the keys to the Cabinet boxes. Albert had succeeded in making himself 'in fact, tho' not in name, Her Majesty's Private Secretary'.[7]

Outside the sheets of the marital bed, the twenty-year-old prince had a clear agenda. His next move was to eliminate the two people who enjoyed the queen's confidence: Lord Melbourne, in effect the previous private secretary, and Baroness Lehzen. Melbourne, who resigned as prime minister after his defeat at the 1841 election, was not really a problem. He wrote harmless letters to the queen from his retirement. Albert's attempt to stop the correspondence was clumsy and ill-judged, especially as this time the queen made no attempt to block the incoming prime minister, Sir Robert Peel.

Far harder to get rid of was Baroness Lehzen, Victoria's former governess, who controlled the court and the queen's private expenditure. Albert became obsessed with 'the old hag', as he called her. He persuaded Victoria that Lehzen was entirely to blame for the rift with her mother, the Duchess of Kent. This was a distortion of the truth – the duchess had abused Victoria cruelly; but relations were restored, and family harmony patched up. According the duchess status as the queen's mother raised the prestige of Albert, who was the duchess's nephew. And Albert brainwashed Victoria into believing that Lehzen had given her a bad upbringing which had 'warped' her character.[8]

*

In January 1842 Victoria and Albert visited Claremont, fourteen miles from Windsor, the home of the couple's uncle Leopold for fifteen years after Charlotte's death. Victoria was recuperating after the birth of her second child, Albert Edward, the Prince of Wales. It snowed heavily, and Albert (with the help of six men) built a snowman twelve feet high, the first Victoria had ever seen. Worried about Vicky, their fourteen-month-old daughter, who was ill at Windsor, the couple cut short their visit and returned home. Victoria wrote in her journal: 'Went at once upstairs, and found poor dear "Pussy" [Vicky] looking thin and pulled down, but she was very pleased to see us.'[9]

What happened next was redacted from the journal by Princess Beatrice, but it's clear that a flaming row ensued. Albert blamed Baroness Lehzen for neglecting the child. This was unfair – Lehzen was not responsible for the day-to-day running of the nursery – but when Victoria said as much, Albert stormed out and refused to speak to her for three days. He sent Victoria angry notes via Baron Stockmar, accusing her of neglecting Vicky: 'take the child away and do as you like,' he wrote, 'and if she dies you will have it on your conscience'.[10] Stockmar sided with Albert, and warned the queen that if she continued to make scenes such as this Albert would be obliged to leave England. At length Victoria capitulated, and agreed that Lehzen should go. She wrote an anguished letter to Stockmar:

> There is often an irritability in me which ... makes me say cross and odious things which I don't believe myself and which I fear hurt Albert but which he should not believe; but

I will strive to conquer it though I knew <u>before</u> I married that this would be a trouble; I therefore wished <u>not</u> to marry, as the two years and a half, when I was completely my own mistress made it difficult for me to control myself and to bend to another's will, but I trust I shall be able to conquer it.

She added: 'Our position is tho' very different to any other married couples. A. is in my house and not I in his. – But I am ready to submit to his wishes as I love him so dearly.'[11]

Victoria had changed. Never before had she spoken of bending or submitting. She had invented a new narrative for herself: she now claimed that her life as queen before Albert had been artificial and superficial, but she was redeemed by her love for him. Later, she destroyed letters from those early years: 'mere amusement, flattery, excitement and mere politics' made it, she wrote, 'the least sensible and satisfactory time in her whole life ... But <u>all</u> changed after '40 ... '.[12] This new Victoria was the creation of Prince Albert.

From 1842, when Victoria was pregnant with her third child, Albert started to attend meetings with ministers. Victoria now talked of 'We' not 'I'. Albert wrote notes of these meetings and corresponded with ministers. She gave him a throne next to hers in the House of Lords. 'He is as much King as She can make him,' remarked Greville. 'All this however does not make him more popular.'[13]

In Winterhalter's painting *The Royal Family in 1846*, Albert and Victoria sit side by side on chairs of state. They wear court evening dress, the blue Garter ribbon on their left shoulders, while their five small children play beside them, giving the painting an unreal air. Victoria thought it 'one of the finest Modern Pictures painted, both as to composition and colouring, and the likenesses are most striking. It is in the style of a Paul Veronese, and has not at all the appearance of "a Family Picture" which is so seldom an agreeable thing.'[14] As head of state, Victoria wears a crown, but Albert's status as head of the family is clearly signalled. He is seated in the presence of the queen, and within the pictorial space he is positioned in front of her. He protects the queen from the outside world; while Victoria stares blankly out of the picture frame, Albert's gaze is fixed on his eldest son, the Prince of Wales. Albert is the dynamic, dominant figure, the man of action, responsible for educating the royal heir as well as the founder of the dynasty.[15]

Albert wrote in 1850 that, as the husband of the queen, it was his role to 'entirely sink his *own individual* existence in that of his wife – that he should aim at no power by himself or for himself – should shun all contention – assume no separate responsibility before the public, but make his position entirely a part of hers – fill up every gap which, as a woman, she would naturally leave in the exercise of her regal functions . . .'. So far, so uncontroversial. This is a definition of the role of the consort as it is understood today. But Albert went on to make large claims – claims which, if he had been a female consort, would have been unthinkable in nineteenth-century Britain. 'As the natural head of her family, superintendent of her household, manager of her private affairs, sole confidential adviser in politics, and only assistant in her communications with the officers of her government he is, besides, the husband of the Queen, the tutor of the royal children, the private secretary of the sovereign, and her permanent minister.'[16] There was a tension here: was Albert Victoria's consort and private secretary, or was he something more? He could hardly be a minister if he was not accountable to Parliament. His role as he understood it amounted to being king in all but name, while Victoria was a merely ornamental sovereign.

At 1 a.m. one night in 1840 a boy named Jones ('In-I-Go Jones') was discovered lying beneath a sofa in a room next to the queen's bedroom at Buckingham Palace. Two years earlier a lad called Cotton had been found in the palace kitchens, where he had been living for twelve months unobserved. Not only was the security of Buckingham Palace so leaky as to be worthless, but the royal household was dysfunctional, chaotic and wasteful. The two officers responsible for the running of the palace were the Lord Steward and the Lord Chamberlain. These were both political appointments, and the work was delegated. Their duties overlapped – it was famously the case that the Lord Steward found the fuel and laid the fire, while the Lord Chamberlain lit it. Albert was a gifted administrator, and, advised by Stockmar, one of his first acts was to overhaul the management of the household. Overall control of the running of the palace was given to a single, resident officer – the Master of the Household. Wasteful expenditure was cut, and perks – such as allowing servants to resell unused candles, which were replaced daily in the public rooms – were scrapped.[17]

The fall of Lord Melbourne left the party-going, pleasure-loving court of Victoria's early reign unprotected. Albert's idea of court life was very different. He thought the court should set a moral example. Camelot it was not. The gaming tables were removed and the wine rationed. Victoria as a young queen was spontaneous and natural, rushing bare-footed to fetch things from Albert's room. Albert, however, was stiff and formal. He tightened the etiquette at court. It was Albert who ruled that no man should sit in the presence of the queen. Maids of honour were forbidden to be seated in Albert's presence, or to speak to him unless spoken to. The conversation was dull. Protocol forbade talking politics or gossip, and wits made the prince uneasy. To protect his reputation as well as his dignity, Albert went everywhere – whether in a carriage or on horseback – accompanied by his equerry. 'He paid no visits in general society.'[18] Nor did the queen.

To the hard-working, early-rising prince, London's late nights were moral pollution. Ill at ease in the company of the aristocracy, who sneered at him as a German beggar, Albert withdrew the royal family from Society. He persuaded Victoria that her enjoyment of London was wrong, and real happiness – the good life – was to be found in the country at Windsor with her beloved husband.

Creating a semi-private space for the royal family was something new. Victoria boasted to Uncle Leopold in 1843 that 'not only <u>no Royal ménage</u> is to be found equal to ours, but <u>no other ménage</u> is to be compared to <u>ours</u>'.[19] Albert's bourgeois style of monarchy had the added advantage that it made the queen popular. As Victoria wrote (again to Leopold, the next year): 'they say <u>no</u> Sovereign <u>was more</u> loved than I am ... and <u>that</u> from our <u>happy domestic home</u> – which gives such a good example'.[20] This domesticity was congenial to her, but it was also prudent. She told Leopold: 'God knows <u>how willingly</u> I would always live with my beloved Albert and our children in the quiet and retirement of private life and not be the constant object of observation and of newspaper articles.'[21] Staying in Brighton at George IV's Pavilion (which she disliked), Victoria was mobbed in the street by shop boys, 'who ran and looked under my bonnet'.[22] Out driving in her carriage with Albert on Constitution Hill, Victoria was shot at by a feeble-minded seventeen-year-old standing in the crowd. He missed. Another attempt was made in the same place by a twenty-year-old lunatic two years later.

To escape the pistols of mad boys and the prying eyes of a newly intrusive public, Albert and Victoria retreated. The Pavilion was sold to Brighton town, and Albert found a new seaside home safely inaccessible on the Isle of Wight. This he bought using the queen's private money – thus deflecting political criticism, as well as underlining that Osborne was the property of the royal family rather than the nation. How 'snug and nice' it was, said Victoria, 'to have a place of <u>one's own</u>, quiet and retired, and free from all Woods and Forests and other charming Departments who really are the plague of one's life'.[23]

A very hot day at Osborne, 30 July 1847. The sea is so calm and blue that it looks, as Albert says, 'like Naples'.[24] The queen drives down to the family's private beach with her maid and steps into the bathing machine. This is a wooden hut, fitted with a changing room and plumbed with a WC, which runs on stone rails and is winched into the sea. Inside the hut the queen undresses, changes into a burka-like concealing bathing dress by the light of two frosted-glass windows high up in the eaves, and descends five wooden steps into the sea. When the sea has concealed her, the machine is removed and she sea-bathes for the first time in her life. 'I thought it delightful till I put my head under the water, when I thought I should be stifled.'[25]

Albert built the house at Osborne – its white-stuccoed Italian campaniles glinting in the sun – with the help of Thomas Cubitt, the architect of Belgravia. Some thought it 'on rather a Londony plan', but to Victoria, 'The liberty, the peace, and retirement we enjoy here, in this lovely country is a <u>real</u> blessing, for which we cannot be sufficiently thankful, – as it has also a most beneficial and calming effect on one's mind and spirits.'[26] After breakfast on the terrace, Victoria spent her mornings painting, and in her watercolours the sun always shines at Osborne.[27] Albert busied himself with tree-planting, landscape gardening, running a model farm and experimenting with sewage treatment. In the evenings they would stand together on the balcony and listen to the song of the nightingale.

With its big plate-glass windows, Osborne was freezing in winter, and Victoria, who disliked heated, stuffy rooms, thrived in the stone-cold halls with their icy draughts while her household shivered. On each chimneypiece, as in all her palaces, there stood a thermometer, set in an ivory obelisk, and her staff were ordered to ensure that the temperature indoors never rose above 60 degrees.[28] In the intimate, interconnecting rooms of the royal suite – which can still be seen today – Victoria and Albert had baths with running hot water which were plumbed to allow the water to drain away. There were water closets too – Victoria was a pioneer of the 'convenience', as she called it, and had them installed in all her palaces.[29] Victoria's ladies, however, dreaded Osborne, especially the long evenings, which were unbearably tedious. Uncoupling the royal family from Society made for a very dull court.

In the first ten years of her marriage, Victoria had seven of her nine children.* Between 1840 and 1850 she spent effectively seven years either being pregnant or lying-in (this lasted about six weeks after the birth). Victoria had 'hated the thought of having children', and didn't want a large family.[30] When she became pregnant with her first child, she wrote: 'I could not be more unhappy; I am really upset about it.'[31] After the baby's birth, she wrote to her uncle Leopold: 'You cannot _really_ wish me to be the "Mamma d'une _nombreuse_ famille".'[32] Within weeks of writing this, she was once more pregnant with her second child.

---

* Vicky, the Princess Royal, born on 21 November 1840; Albert Edward (Bertie), Prince of Wales, 9 November 1841; Alice, 25 April 1843; Alfred, 6 August 1844; Helena, 25 May 1846; Louise, 18 March 1848; Arthur, 1 May 1850. Her eighth child, Leopold, was born on 7 April 1853 and Beatrice, the youngest, on 14 April 1857.

Victoria's serial pregnancies suited Albert. He could get on with the business of ruling, and a large family fitted his idea of domestic monarchy – as well as offering opportunities for dynasty-building. Victoria, however, considered that the first two years of her marriage were 'utterly spoilt' by childbearing. Pregnancy, she wrote, was 'the shadow side' of marriage. 'Without that ... if one has a husband one worships! It is a foretaste of heaven.' When her daughter Vicky gushed about her pride in giving birth to an immortal soul, Victoria snapped back: 'I think much more of our being a cow or a dog at such moments; when our poor nature becomes so very animal and unecstatic.' Babies, she wrote, 'are mere little plants for the first six months'. She thought them 'frightful when undressed' with 'their big body and little limbs and that terrible frog-like action.'[33]

These blisteringly candid letters were written in 1858. How far they reflect Victoria's feelings at the time her children were born is hard to tell. As was normal for high-status women, Victoria didn't breastfeed her 'little plants', and, partly because she was not lactating, her children were spaced closely together. The appointment of a wet-nurse for the Prince of Wales was welcomed by *The Times*, which reported how Mrs Brough, the wife of a royal servant from Claremont, had joined the women – many of them 'ladies of ample means' – queuing for the job at Buckingham Palace.*[34]

---

* The job was very well paid. Vicky's wet-nurse earned £500: Mrs Brough got £1,000 for the Prince of Wales. Victoria found her 'morose, ill tempered and stupid': she later went mad and murdered all her six children. (RA VIC/MAIN/QVJ [W] 13 June 1854 [Princess Beatrice's copies].)

When medical opinion turned against wet-nursing in the 1860s and doctors urged mothers to breastfeed, the queen remained adamantly opposed. She was furious when her daughters rebelled and breastfed their babies, declaring that 'a <u>Child can never be as well</u> nursed by a <u>lady</u> of <u>rank</u> and <u>nervous</u> and <u>refined temperament</u> – for the <u>less feeling</u> and the <u>more like</u> an <u>animal</u> the <u>wet nurse is</u>, the <u>better</u> for the child.'[35]

Victoria resented 'the shadow side' of marriage because it got in the way of her nights with Albert, not because it prevented her from doing her job as queen. She told Vicky: 'I owe everything to dearest Papa. He was my father, my protector, my guide and adviser in all and everything, my mother (I might almost say) as well as my husband. I suppose no one was ever so completely altered in every way as I was by dearest Papa's blessed influence.'[36] Albert was her mother – a word which reveals much about Victoria's relationship with her own mother – and she was his child. She was emotionally dependent upon him, and sexually in thrall to him.

She now believed that being Queen Regnant was 'an anomalous position'. Women were not meant to govern. 'Though dear Papa, God knows, does everything – it is a reversal of the right order of things which distresses me much and which no one, but such a perfection, such an angel as he is – could bear and carry through.'[37]

Victoria the 'resolute little tit' had reinvented herself as the angel in the home, but she knew little of family life. Albert had been even more starved of parental affection. Primed by Stockmar, Albert opined that the chief aim of the royal parents was to make the children – and particularly the Prince of Wales – as unlike as possible any of Victoria's 'wicked uncles'. This was disingenuous. Albert's own father (as Greville pointed out) was 'by far the worst of the family' – even worse than the Hanoverians.[38]

Victoria declared that 'the children should be brought up as <u>simply</u> and in as domestic a way as possible; that (not interfering with their lessons) they should be as <u>much as possible</u> with their parents'.[39] She doted on Vicky, a precocious little girl, who was endlessly dressed up and kept up late and had her clever sayings repeated by the court. Bertie, 'the Boy', whose birth she had resented, and who was not as quick as his sister, was not adored. In her sketchbook Victoria made pencil drawings and watercolours of her children, often wearing fancy dress or standing in groups. Tellingly, perhaps, Albert is absent from these family sketches. There is another absence: from about the age of ten, Bertie, the difficult and disappointing eldest son, disappears from the sketchbook. The album of family sketches stops in 1861, when Albert died. As Marina Warner wrote: 'The imagery of family pleasure was not exactly hollow for her, but it was borrowed, and she needed Albert beside her to mastermind it.'[40]

A fortnight after the birth of her fifth child, Helena, in the summer of 1846, Victoria resumed writing her journal. Albert, she recorded, had been with her – as he always was – throughout the birth, holding her hands and fanning her, and during her lying-in he read to her every evening. The state of politics was very worrying. Peel, the couple's favourite minister, had just passed the bill repealing the Corn Laws, and his government was on the brink of falling. But, the queen recorded: 'Really when one is so happy and blessed in one's home life, as I am, Politics (provided my Country is safe) must take only a 2nd place.'[41]

5
The Queen's Mind

The opening of the Great Exhibition in Hyde Park, 1 May 1851. Victoria and Albert drive in a procession of nine state carriages through the packed crowds to Joseph Paxton's Crystal Palace. This is Albert's project, and to Victoria, making her entrance into the gigantic glass edifice filled with cheering people 'gave a sensation I shall never forget and I felt much moved'.[1] 'It was', she told her uncle, 'the <u>happiest, proudest</u> day in my life, and I can think of nothing else. Albert's dearest name is immortalised with this <u>great</u> conception, <u>his</u> own, and my <u>own</u> dear country <u>showed</u> she was <u>worthy</u> of it.'[2] For once, the country had behaved itself.

The country's love affair with Albert was short-lived. In the winter of 1853–4, as anti-Russian fever gripped the nation in the run-up to the Crimean War, Albert was engulfed in a storm of vicious press attacks. He was vilified for meddling in foreign policy. It was claimed, with some justice, that he had waged a vendetta against the foreign secretary, Lord Palmerston, culminating in the latter's dismissal two years before. Albert was accused, unfairly, of pursuing a pro-German foreign policy, which was dictated by Coburg, dubbed by the radical press 'this beggarly, dirty, poverty-stricken, hole-and-corner Duchy'. Wild rumours spread that Albert had been sent to the Tower of London, and crowds gathered to await his committal. His popularity slumped to a low point from which it never really recovered. Albert was bruised and shocked but unrepentant. How was it, he wondered, that the nation had not discovered that 'an important personage has during all [this] time taken a part in governing them'?[3]

What Albert believed the role of the sovereign to be can be seen from an extraordinary memorandum composed at the height of this crisis by Baron Stockmar. By now a wizened hypochondriac who felt the cold at Windsor so badly that he was granted special permission not to wear tights, Stockmar continued to act as Albert's political adviser. Pointing to the decline in the power of the sovereign that had occurred since the 1832 Reform Act, Stockmar urged that the crown must fight back to regain what it had lost. The role of the monarch was that of a 'permanent Premier, who takes rank above the temporary head of the Cabinet, and in matters of discipline exercises supreme authority'. Albert replied: 'I heartily agree with every word you say.'[4]

Stockmar called this 'constitutional monarchy', but he didn't understand the term in the way that the British did. Indeed, his knowledge of the British constitution was alarmingly shaky. But Stockmar's teaching had one good effect. If the monarch was to act as Stockmar envisaged – as a permanent prime minister – she or he must be non-partisan. After the fall of the Tory prime minister Robert Peel, who had become a royal favourite, Albert followed a policy of strict political neutrality. In this sense, he anticipated the modern British monarchy. But in his understanding of the role and powers of the crown, Albert's ideas were far from modern – rather closer to an eighteenth-century enlightened despot in a small German state than Britain in the age of reform.[5]

Here is an account, written in 1857, of the working of the monarchy of Albert and Victoria:

> ... the Queen in her own name, but under the inspiration of the Prince ... held each Minister to the discharge of his duty and his responsibility to her, and constantly desired to be furnished with accurate and detailed information about all important matters, keeping a record of all the reports that were made to her, and constantly recurring to them, e.g. she would desire to know what the state of the Navy was, and what ships were in readiness for active service, and generally the state of each, ordering returns to be submitted to her from all the arsenals and dockyards, and again weeks or months afterwards referring to these returns, and desiring to have everything relating to them explained and accounted for, and so throughout every department ... This is what none of her Predecessors ever did, and it is in fact the act of Albert, who is to all intents and purposes King, only acting entirely in her name.[6]

Buckingham Palace under Albert was effectively a department of government, performing a role not unlike the Cabinet Office in the twentieth century. The monarchy was a secretariat which kept a vigilant watch over all departments of government. This imposed a massive burden of work. Albert grasped the simple truth that information is power, and he was ahead of his time in devising clever systems to organize it – so increasing the load even more.

From the mid 1840s, Albert abandoned the conventional method of filing the queen's correspondence by sender, and – with Stockmar at his side – he began to arrange it by subject. This enabled him to access information far more efficiently, but – in those pre-computer days – it meant that letters which ranged over several topics had to be copied. Because these letters came from the secret Cabinet boxes to which only Albert – and not his staff – had the key, he alone (or so he thought) could make the copies. No one but Albert could transcribe the near-sacred letters written by the queen (most of which he had drafted in the first place). Only he could keep notes of the royal couple's meetings with ministers or make extracts of Foreign Office despatches.[7]

Albert was trapped on a treadmill of his own devising, endlessly copying to keep pace with the ever-increasing flow of government documents. This was a monarchy that ran on ink. Delegation seems not to have occurred to him. He had become like Bob Cratchit in Dickens's *A Christmas Carol*, a slave to his desk, except that he wore a Garter ribbon – the nation's grandest clerk. On winter mornings he rose before dawn and worked in the chill gloom by the light of his green German reading lamp. The handsome youth of fifteen years before was at thirty-five a middle-aged man – stooping, fleshy and balding. As Lytton Strachey waspishly observed, 'Unkind critics, who had once compared Albert to an operatic tenor, might have remarked that there was something of the butler about him now.'[8]

Victoria observed that Albert had become 'really a <u>terrible</u> man of business; I think it takes a little off from the gentleness of his character, and makes him so preoccupied'. But she was thankful to be relieved of what she considered to be the masculine work of politics. She had become a puppet – or perhaps one of the dolls that she had dressed and played with as a child. She mouthed the briefings provided by the beloved prince, and at dinners with ministers he could be heard prompting her in German. Seated beside him at her writing desk, she spent hours copying out the drafts that Albert composed. Observant ministers noticed the worrying contrast between the queen's business letters, which were drafted by Albert and were always clear and well-written, and the notes she scrawled herself, which were 'slovenly', with 'many words underscored . . . full of scratches and corrections'.[9] Without the prince where would she be?

The queen was at Balmoral, her new home in Scotland, on 10 September 1855, sitting quietly after dinner, when at 10.30 a telegram arrived announcing the fall of Sebastopol. The defeat of the Russian armies in the Crimea after a siege lasting twelve months was the news for which she had been anxiously waiting. It meant that victory for the British and the French was assured. Albert and the gentlemen sallied forth at once to celebrate at the cairn on the top of the hill. The bonfire blazed, the whisky flowed, the pipes swirled and the Highlanders danced and shouted and fired off guns – a wild, heathen scene.[10]

During the Crimean War, Albert worked more feverishly than ever, filling fifty volumes with papers, but he remained stiff and distant. At a reception for a victorious Crimean general, Albert 'stood bolt upright, didn't shake hands, just nodded', making everyone 'furious'.[11] Victoria, by contrast, found a new role – perhaps she discovered a vocation – as a warrior queen, and she reached out to her people in a way she had never done before. At the time of the 1848 Revolutions, when her brother sovereigns were toppling from their thrones, she had written: '<u>Great</u> events make me quiet and calm, and little trifles fidget me and irritate my nerves.' Galvanized by the Crimean War, Victoria demanded military information from her generals, bullied the government to build better military hospitals and barracks, insisted on signing the commission of every officer and gave out all medals herself.* Touching the rough hands of wounded private soldiers taught her compassion. She felt they were '<u>my own children</u>; my heart beats for <u>them</u>'.[12] Never had she regretted more being a woman. Echoing Elizabeth I, a queen she did not admire, she declared: 'I regret exceedingly not to be a man and to be able to fight in the war.'†[13]

Victoria and Albert had moved into the new house which Albert built at Balmoral only days before Sebastopol fell.

---

* The first batch of sixty-two Victoria Crosses, which both Victoria and Albert helped to design, were awarded by her in 1856.
† Victoria claimed to prefer Mary Queen of Scots to Elizabeth. 'I have no sympathy with my great predecessor,' she wrote, 'descended as I am from her rival Queen, whom she so cruelly sacrificed'. (QV to Rosebery, 21 July 1887, in QVL, 3rd series, vol. 1, p. 341.)

Creating a royal residence in Scotland was good for the monarchy; it forged a loyalty to the crown of the sort that was worryingly lacking in Ireland. Since 1848 Victoria and Albert had spent the early autumn at the small gentry house of Balmoral, where they lived very simply. With the new castle, built in the baronial gothic style, the German royal pair created a fantasy of invented Scottish tradition. Albert designed his own Balmoral tartan – grey with a red sett – and also the Victoria tartan, with a white stripe. There were tartan carpets, tartan chair covers, tartan curtains and even tartan linoleum in the servants' quarters. Albert sported a kilt in Royal Stuart (for which, noted one maid of honour, 'he was rather too fat and substantial'), Victoria was swathed in satin tartan, the little princes wore full Highland dress and after dinner reel-dancing was impossible to avoid.[14]

For Albert, the 'primitive, yet romantic, mountain life' reminded him of his youth in the Thuringian forest.[15] He was an enthusiastic stalker of deer, but an indifferent marksman, and the casual brutality of his shooting – wounding animals or taking pot-shots at deer out of the queen's carriage windows – flouted British standards of sportsmanship. People muttered about his German methods; but perhaps shooting gave vent to a streak of violence in his nature buried deep beneath the carefully cultivated exterior of the civilized prince.[16]

For Victoria, Balmoral, like Osborne, brought freedom and an escape from the purdah of Buckingham Palace. What a joy it was to play the part of a Highland gentlewoman, visiting the cottagers unannounced, taking tea and bringing gifts of warm petticoats for the old women. She valued especially the Highlanders' straightforwardness and lack of deference. 'One of the great advantages and charms of our life at Balmoral is the means it gives us of free intercourse with the people,' she wrote. 'We stand so high and particularly I do, that I am constantly as it were cut off from contact with those of an inferior class.'[17]

Victoria's ninth and last child, Beatrice, was born in April 1857. The birth itself was easy, aided by the new wonder drug of chloroform, and the thirty-seven-year-old mother declared: 'I have felt better and stronger this time than I have ever done before.'[18] But the pregnancy was scarred by 'nerves' and tantrums. Whenever Victoria made a scene, Albert calmly walked away. Afterwards, he wrote her patronizing notes, reporting on her as if she were a patient. 'I am trying to keep out of your way until your better feelings have returned and you have gained control of yourself,' he told her.[19]

There had been hysterical scenes too after the birth of Leopold, Victoria's eighth child, in 1853. Albert wrote her cold letters full of recriminations. 'If you are violent I have no other choice but to leave you . . . and retire to my room in order to give you time to recover yourself, then you follow me to renew the dispute and have it all out,' he wrote in 1853. The nervous attacks occurred distressingly often, even when Victoria was not pregnant. Albert noted 'four weeks of unbroken success in the hard struggle for self-control' as a mark of progress in 1855.[20] In 1856 the queen's doctor Sir James Clark recorded his fears for her sanity.

'Regarding the Queen's mind, unless she is kept quiet and still amused, the time will come when she is in danger,' he wrote. 'Much depends on the Prince's management.'[21]

Always in the background was the fear that the queen had inherited the madness of her grandfather, George III. This certainly was Stockmar's concern, and he impressed it upon Albert. In 1858 Greville noted that Albert 'was completely cowed, and the Q. so excitable that the P. lived in perpetual terror of bringing on the hereditary malady'.[22]

Was Victoria mad? The madness of George III was diagnosed in the 1960s by Ida Macalpine and Richard Hunter, a mother and son team of psychiatrists, as porphyria, an inherited metabolic condition, which causes bouts of insanity, acute illness and – fittingly for royal persons – purple urine. This diagnosis has been challenged by Timothy Peters, a porphyria clinician. Using twenty-first-century diagnostic techniques, he has proposed that George III suffered from bipolar disorder with manic episodes.*[23] Historians turn out to have been all too gullible in swallowing the porphyria theory, but it would also probably be a mistake to accept the bipolar theory as gospel. Current thinking suggests that George III's malady was not hereditary. Nor was Victoria insane. But she was prone to 'nerves' and violent temper tantrums, and the tensions in her relationship with Albert made this worse.

---

* The porphyria diagnosis was based on a wide range of non-specific symptoms. The symptom that clinched the Macalpine/Hunter diagnosis was George III's purple-blue urine, but this may have been caused by medicine made from gentians.

The basis of the marriage was Victoria's subservience to Albert. She was, as we have seen, his 'Child', his patient and his pupil, intellectually and morally his inferior. She must always agree with him, in order to avoid exercising her sovereign power over the man she had vowed to obey. In exchange, she demanded his constant, undivided attention. When he was away she felt 'quite paralysed'.[24]

Sustaining an unequal, contrived relationship such as this could never be easy, but some problems were possible to fix. One was the anomaly – in Victoria's eyes – that, as the husband of the queen, Albert's rank was inferior to hers, but in English law a husband enjoyed power over his wife. In 1857 she conferred on him the title of Prince Consort, which gave him precedence over everyone except her.[25] It also ensured that their sons could not claim higher rank than Albert as a mere German prince.

Far harder to change was her character. Victoria did her best to please Albert by attempting to teach herself self-control. She kept a notebook in which she charted her backslidings – the moments of misery caused by 'my foolish sensitiveness and irritability', giving 'annoyance to that most perfect of human beings my adored husband'. She confessed: 'Again and again have I conquered this susceptibility – have formed the best of resolutions and <u>again</u> it returns.'[26] 'Have <u>I</u> improved as <u>much</u> as I ought?' she asked herself. 'I fear <u>not</u> ... To my beloved and perfect husband, I fear also, I have been a great trouble, and this <u>also</u>, I pray to be helped and assisted in <u>no</u> longer being. I have <u>great</u> difficulties in my <u>own</u> poor temper, violent feelings, disposition and <u>position</u>, which tend to make one selfish!'[27]

Albert perceived that Victoria's wilfulness had never been checked, and no one had taught her to control her temper. He issued her with a 'very good certificate' of 'improvement': 'controlling your feelings is your great task, you say, in life'.[28] By treating her as a pupil with himself as moral tutor or priest, he succeeded only in making her feel inadequate. Stockmar worsened matters by pathologizing Victoria's rages and diagnosing the 'hereditary malady'. This allowed Albert to avoid confrontation, which was in any case his natural inclination. As Elizabeth Longford wrote: 'Following him from room to room [Albert] saw, not a perfectly sane though angry Victoria, but the mad ghost of George III.'[29] She was in danger of becoming like the mad Mrs Rochester in Charlotte Brontë's *Jane Eyre* – a madwoman in the attic, ostracized because she did not conform to the Victorian paradigm of sweetness and light.*

After the birth of Beatrice, Sir James Clark warned Victoria that another pregnancy would endanger her (mental) health. 'Oh, Sir James,' she is alleged to have replied, 'can I have no more fun in bed?'[30] Queen and Consort continued to share the marital bed.[31] But there were no more pregnancies, and this suggests a regime of sexual abstinence – a change which Victoria must have found hard to bear. In spite – or perhaps because – of Albert's sleeping costume of long white drawers that enclosed his feet, and regardless of the

---

* Victoria read *Jane Eyre* aloud to Albert in 1858; she found it 'intensely interesting' and 'quite creepy'. (RA VIC/MAIN/QVJ [W] 13, 21 May 1858 [Princess Beatrice's copies].)

maid who always slept on a sofa outside her bedroom door, Victoria was, as she wrote, still 'ardent'.[32]

Bruised by his unpopularity, depressed and lonely – he had no English friends – Albert took refuge in work. He complained that he was a donkey on a treadmill, but business had become a psychological necessity to him. His work was intended to protect Victoria and shield her from overtaxing her mind, but it had the opposite effect: it made her mental state worse, because it gave him reason for avoiding her company.

Victoria's intense, self-absorbed marriage left little space for her children. She frankly confessed that, when Albert was away for the day, 'I find no especial pleasure or compensation in the company of the elder children.'[33] She considered that it was her role to correct and scold her children and order them about. This 'aggressive' system of parenting meant they must not become too intimate. As Albert observed, 'It is not possible to be on happy friendly terms with people you have just been scolding.'[34] Victoria knew no other way; she was replicating the difficult relationship she had had with her own mother.

Vicky and Bertie, the two elder children, were each – in their different ways – a source of anxiety to Victoria. In adolescence, both were forced to conform to the appalling pressures imposed by Albert's dynastic strategy. While Vicky complied, Bertie rebelled. Victoria's responses show her at her best as a mother and at her worst.

Vicky, who was something of a child prodigy, had always

been especially close to her father. In 1855 the fourteen-year-old princess became engaged to Frederick William, known as Fritz, eleven years her senior, the heir apparent to the King of Prussia. This marriage, uniting the crowns of Britain and Prussia, had been planned by Albert ever since Vicky was a baby, and he especially was overjoyed. Each evening he gave Vicky tutorials in politics, and Victoria, who was intimidated by her daughter's cleverness, felt excluded. Resentful of Vicky for monopolizing Albert's attention, she made no attempt to stop her from making a child-marriage, and then she blamed herself for letting it happen.[35]

Once Vicky married and left England for Berlin, Victoria was 'in a constant fidget' to know everything and deluged her daughter with letters.[36] When Victoria learned that Vicky, aged seventeen, was pregnant, she wrote deploring the 'horrid news'.[37] This was hardly the reaction that Vicky wanted to hear, but Victoria's comment was charged with remorse. Vicky's dangerous teenage pregnancy was in a way her fault, and she dreaded her daughter's subjection to the 'shadow side' of marriage. Vicky nearly died giving birth to her first child (later Kaiser Wilhelm II), confirming Victoria's worst fears.

Primed by Stockmar – on whose bad advice he was blindly dependent – Albert scolded Victoria for writing too often to Vicky. The queen, claimed her critics, was attempting to control Vicky's life in Prussia as she had done when she was a child at home, and her nagging, bossy letters put an unreasonable burden on the poor princess, who was worried sick because she was obliged to answer her mother's constant bombardment.[38] But what Victoria wanted was not to control Vicky, but to have a conversation with her – tell me, she urged, about your feelings, about the little interior details.[39]

Letter-writing was the glue that kept dynasties together, but this mother-daughter correspondence was far more than a dutiful exchange. In the twice-weekly letters that she penned to Vicky (which were not read by Albert) she wrote as she talked – spontaneously, often vehemently, revealing her inner feelings without restraint. She grew closer to her daughter than she had ever been when Vicky was at home. No longer the scolding mother and sovereign, she wrote as one married woman to another. 'Marriage', as the editor of the letters wrote, 'transformed everything: it was the grand equaliser.' And Victoria was lonely. Albert's withdrawal of the family into an inner citadel left her with few women friends. Writing to Vicky filled a void in her life. Far from being a chore, 'our dear correspondence' answered an emotional need for the mother, as well as the daughter, a lonely princess in a foreign court.[40]

On the day of Bertie's confirmation – an important rite of passage for her sixteen-year-old son – Victoria wrote in her private notebook: 'Oh! <u>how</u> earnestly <u>did</u> I pray to God for <u>help</u> and for blessings on that poor boy, who causes us from his character and his position such <u>immense anxiety</u>!'[41]

It was Bertie's destiny as heir apparent to carry on Albert's work. Albert believed that 'the exaltation of Royalty' depended on the 'personal character of the Sovereign'. 'When a person enjoys complete confidence, we desire for him more power also and influence in the conduct of affairs.'[42] Hard work and braininess were the reasons for Albert's success and Albert, who was responsible for Bertie's education, tried to reproduce his own schooling for his son. From the age of six, Bertie took his lessons alone with a tutor, following a tightly packed timetable devised by his father (Albert liked nothing better than composing timetables). The experiment was a disaster. Bertie raged and stamped and screamed and learned very little. His tutors despaired. The reason, thought Albert, was not the system – it never seems to have occurred to him that solitary lessons were unsuited to his son's extrovert nature. The problem must be the boy himself. Advised as always by Stockmar, Albert called in the phrenologists or brain doctors. They calibrated the bumps on his head and diagnosed subnormal intelligence. Bertie was a patient – like his mother, he had special needs. Stockmar whispered darkly about the Hanoverian madness resurfacing once more.[43]

Victoria exhorted Bertie to model himself on Albert, the perfect being:

> You none of you can <u>ever</u> be proud enough of being the <u>child</u> of <u>such</u> a father, who has <u>not</u> his equal in this World! So great, so good, so faultless. Try <u>all</u> of you to follow in his footsteps and don't be discouraged – for to be <u>really</u> in everything like him – <u>none</u> of you I am sure ever will be; try therefore to be like him in some points and you will have gained a <u>great</u> <u>deal</u>.[44]

But Bertie seemed not to resemble his father at all. On the contrary, he was, as Stockmar pointed out, an exaggerated copy of his mother. Even Victoria had the insight to describe him as her 'caricature'.[45] Bertie seemed to have inherited all the characteristics Victoria was most anxious to rid herself of. Her quarrels with Bertie reflected her own lack of self-worth.

Victoria's antipathy towards Bertie was visceral. Forthright and trenchant, she laid into her son and complained vigorously about him behind his back. Bertie received regular broadsides from his mother, attacking him for dawdling, for laziness, for his hairstyle, for his self-indulgent habit of lying on a sofa. To Vicky she objected that he was dull and stupid. 'Handsome I cannot think him, with that painfully small and narrow head, those immense features and total want of chin.'[46] In her private notebook she agonized about Bertie's woeful inadequacy:

> He has a good heart and is very affte [*sic*], and at bottom very truthful, but his intellect alas! is weak which is <u>not</u> his fault but, what <u>is</u> his fault <u>is</u> his shocking laziness, which I fear has been far too much indulged, and which goes so far that he listens to nothing you tell him or teach him or what is said before him, but seems in a sort of dreaminess, which alarms <u>us</u> for his <u>brain</u>. He profits by nothing he learns, gives way to temper, very bad <u>manners</u> and great insubordination, all <u>most dangerous</u> qualities for his position . . .[47]

Victoria showed no remorse, nor did she make any attempt to conceal her feelings. Albert's attempt to domesticate and reform his wife – to tame the shrew – had only succeeded in directing her turbulent emotions towards her eldest son.

6
Alone

Windsor Castle, 7 December 1861, 8 a.m. Victoria has endured four of the worst nights of her life. In a state of unbearable anxiety, she has lain awake listening as her sick husband wanders restlessly from room to room of the royal apartments. Albert's illness has dragged on for four weeks now. This morning when she comes to his sitting room she finds him dressed and sitting in an armchair, but weak and exhausted. Again and again he asks her what his illness can be. He tells her that while he lay awake in the winter dawn he heard the little birds, and he was reminded of listening to the birds at the Rosenau as a child. This upsets her greatly. 'I went to my room, and felt as if my heart must break.'

Later that morning, the doctors tell Victoria that an eruption or rash has appeared on Albert's stomach. This is the sign they have been looking for: proof positive that he is suffering from typhoid fever. The fever will now run its course; it usually lasts a month. Though she feels her heart must burst, Victoria allows herself to be reassured – one of the royal doctors, William Jenner, is after all the country's foremost authority on fever. 'I seem to live in a dreadful dream,' she writes. As she sits beside the bed watching her 'angel', the tears fall fast – she thinks of the 'utter ship-wreck' of their plans. When she asks the doctors what caused this illness, they reply: 'Great worry and far too hard work for too long.'[1]

A week later, on 14 December, when Victoria entered Albert's room at 7 a.m. she found the candles burnt down to their sockets and the doctors looking anxious. Though she had received optimistic reports through the night, she knew at once that death was near. 'I can never forget how beautiful my darling looked,' she wrote. Albert lay with his face lit up by the early sun, his eyes unusually bright and 'not taking notice of me'.[2] He died at ten minutes to eleven that night.

What killed Prince Albert? is a question that is still unanswered. The doctors diagnosed typhoid but, in spite of Jenner's expertise, the symptoms do not exactly fit. The immediate cause of death was pneumonia. The *Lancet* suggested that he might have died of 'ulcerative perforation of the bowel'.[3] Victoria forbade an autopsy, and no medical report was published. Since the 1970s biographers have speculated that Albert was weakened by an underlying illness. It has sometimes been suggested that he died of stomach cancer. A more recent theory is that he was a victim of Crohn's Disease.[4]

Albert was undeniably in poor health. For the past two or three years he had suffered from frequent and increasingly severe 'stomach attacks', characterized by violent shivering, rheumatic pains, sickness and diarrhoea. He had bouts of insomnia and depression. He had told Victoria that he did not cling to life: 'I feel that I should make no struggle if I were ill – that I should give it up at once.' Victoria, however, chose to ignore or deny Albert's symptoms. She scolded him for his 'miserable face' and for making no effort to get well. For her, therefore, his death came as a sudden blow, brutal and incomprehensible. Encouraged by the doctors, Victoria made sense of it by blaming 'a great sorrow and worry'.[5]

The 'worry' was what Victoria – speaking apocalyptically – called Bertie's fall. The story of how the nineteen-year-old prince had lost his virginity to a courtesan named Nellie Clifden while on military exercises with the Grenadier Guards at the Curragh in Ireland came as a thunderbolt to Prince Albert. 'Oh! that face, that heavenly face of woe and sorrow,' wrote Victoria.[6] Albert told his son that his fall had caused 'the greatest pain I have yet felt in this life', and in November 1861 he wrote him a hysterical letter, insinuating that he had endangered the future of the dynasty.[7] Victoria, blinded by devotion, failed to see that the really worrying thing was not Bertie's scrape but Albert's reaction, which was disproportionate, even unhinged.

In spite of feeling wretchedly ill, Albert insisted on going to have it out with Bertie at Cambridge, getting soaked to the skin. Victoria later admitted that Albert 'had quite forgiven him and had come away from Madingley [Cambridge] much happier than he had gone down', but her own anger with Bertie was unabated.[8] When Albert died three weeks later, Victoria, desperately in need of a narrative, accused her son of causing Albert's death. Bertie's fall – that 'sad stain' – became a fixation. Her dislike of her son turned to physical revulsion. 'Oh! that boy – much as I pity I never can or shall look at him without a shudder.'[9]

The death of the Prince Consort plunged Victoria into the deepest crisis of her life. The image of the widow swathed in black crêpe and prostrated by grief has diverted attention from the realities of her position. In fact, her strengths were considerable. In spite – or rather because – of her loss, she was utterly determined to carry on Albert's work. 'I will, I <u>will</u> do my duty,' she was heard to mutter as the special train bore her to Osborne, away from Windsor and her last sight of Albert's body.[10] Albert left the monarchy in a far better state than he found it: financially sound, the succession assured, the household and bureaucracy reformed. The death of the prince, who was disliked as a German beggar and a meddler, boosted the queen's popularity; the pathos of her suffering endeared her to her people.[11] Victoria's weakness was her gender. A poorly educated woman in a political world of alpha males with Oxford firsts, she had no hope of competing on equal terms, as Albert had done. She had grown so used to relying on him that she had lost confidence in her own abilities. Albert had indeed been her private secretary, and she now had no one. As a widow she was more reluctant than ever to appear in public.

Albert's death, however, presented the queen with opportunities, if she could but see them. 'A few years more, and we should have had, in practice, an absolute monarchy,' said Disraeli.[12] Albert's interventionism had been tolerated only because post-1846 was a period of political flux, of hung parliaments and coalition governments. Once the two-party system revived, as it did after 1867, Albert's methods risked bringing the crown into conflict with Parliament. His death facilitated the sovereign's retreat from politics. The modern role of constitutional monarch is arguably better suited to a female sovereign – a conciliatory wisdom figure, rather than a working ruler. But Victoria's gender also made her vulnerable to threats, notably the demand that she should abdicate in favour of her son. If she was to counter these threats – and prevent the rise of republican opposition – she must not allow her private sorrow to overwhelm her public duty. Again, her role as a woman was in conflict with her vocation as queen.

No one could accuse Victoria of repressing her grief. In heavily black-bordered letters, she wrote endlessly and obsessively about the dreary emptiness of her existence without Albert. What was the foreign secretary to make of a business letter from H. M. which began: 'The things of this world are of no interest to the Queen . . . for her thoughts are fixed above.'[13] She went out walking 'as if in a dream, thinking and thinking till she was in a sort of stupor always expecting him at every turn and in every room'.[14] At night she slept clasping Albert's nightshirt with a cast of his hand in easy reach. At Windsor and at Osborne his rooms were kept as shrines, supplied daily with fresh flowers and hot water, his pen upon the open blotting book. At Balmoral, 'the stags' heads – the rooms – blessed, darling Papa's room – then his coats – his caps – kilts – all, all convulsed my poor shattered frame!'.[15] She filled her sketchbook with watercolours of the 'wild, grim, solitary mountains', empty now of the people she had once drawn, as if the landscape itself had been widowed. She expected to die imminently, which made it hard to plan for the future – the Queen of Prussia was asked to stay, 'if I am still alive'.[16] Her one consolation was the prospect of rejoining the prince, and in the meantime she communed with him in his *Sterbezimmer* or death chamber. Soon after his death she began to plan the mausoleum at Frogmore, which was his memorial. She was tormented by physical passion. 'I could go mad from the desire and longing,' she wrote. 'I am alas! not old – and my feelings are strong and warm.'[17]

Her household feared she was losing her reason. She herself said grief was driving her mad. Perhaps she was right. Her morbid obsession with Albert *was* abnormal. Even by the standards of the Victorians, who made a cult of death and mourning, her grieving was exceptional. Victoria's grief was pathological, a form of mental illness: she was incapacitated by her loss and fixated by it, and she suffered from severe depression which took years to lift.[18]

Albert's sudden death came at a time when Victoria was anyway in a fragile state. Her mother's death, only nine months earlier, had plunged her into a sort of breakdown. Victoria's relationship with her mother had never been close, and after her accession they had been estranged, but this made the duchess's death a hard blow for her to bear. She felt guilty that she had never loved her mother enough. When she read the little notes that her mother wrote to her as a child, she had been overcome by remorse. Encouraged by Albert, she had abandoned herself to an orgy of grief, and rumours spread about her mental state.[19]

Infantilized by Albert, his death (but not her mother's) made her feel 'like a child that has lost its mother'.[20] She withdrew into seclusion. Her children were no comfort to her. She insisted on dining alone, as laughter and loud talk upset her. The monarchy moved from London to Windsor. Buckingham Palace stood empty, shrouded in dust sheets. 'I never can live there again.'[21] During the remaining forty years of her reign, she slept perhaps two or three nights a year there. She spent long periods at Osborne and Balmoral, the retreats which Albert had created, and for a long time retired from all state ceremonies and court functions. Not until 1868 did she appear at a court drawing room. A wag posted a bill outside Buckingham Palace: 'These commanding premises to be let or sold in consequence of the late occupant's declining business.'[22]

Grief had its uses, however. After two and a half years, a leader appeared in *The Times*, expressing the hope of seeing the queen in public. Victoria took the extraordinary step of replying herself. To call upon her, overwhelmed as she was with public work, to undergo in addition the fatigue of 'mere' state ceremonies was to risk disabling her altogether, she wrote.[23] When Earl Russell was bold enough to invite her to open Parliament in 1865, she replied that it was 'totally out of the question'. 'Her nerves are so shattered that any emotion, any discussion, any exertion' would entail 'a succession of moral shocks as well as very great fatigue'.[24] She never ceased to lament her wretched nerves and broken health. For medicinal purposes, she drank her claret laced with whisky. She put on weight. In 1863 she weighed 11 stone 8 pounds.*[25] She herself admitted that 'she was afraid of getting too well – as if it were a crime'.[26] A threatened Fenian (Irish terrorist) attack was brushed aside by the queen. Showing admirable fortitude, she refused to panic. But any request that she should appear in public was met by what was effectively a sick note from the obliging Dr Jenner.

House of Lords, 6 February 1866. Victoria has at last agreed to open Parliament for the first time since Albert's death. She dreads the ordeal as if it were an execution: 'the spectacle of a poor, broken-hearted widow, nervous and shrinking, dragged in <u>deep mourning</u> ALONE <u>in</u> STATE as a <u>Show</u>'.[27] Terribly nervous and agitated, she has eaten no luncheon. No prima donna could have masterminded the choreography of widowhood better than she. There must be no state coach. Nor will she don the Imperial State Crown, as its brilliant gems would give the lie to her grief.†　She wears her ordinary black evening gown and a white

---

* This weight gives her a BMI of 32.72, which is at the lower end of the obese range. In 1838 she had weighed 8 stone 13 pounds: see footnote, p. 22.

† Victoria never wore the Imperial State Crown after 1861. In 1870 she commissioned the exquisite Small Diamond Crown, set with 1,000 diamonds (colourless and therefore appropriate for mourning), which she wore perched on her head over her white widow's veil.

widow's cap (a reference to the executed Mary Queen of Scots), with a diamond and sapphire coronet. She sits alone, a stout, red-faced figure, on her throne in the House of Lords. Her crimson robes are draped over Albert's empty chair, like a discarded skin. Throughout the ceremony, she stares at the ground as if in melancholy meditation, her face set and expressionless while the Lord Chancellor reads the speech.[28]

Victoria opened Parliament only seven times after 1861 – in 1866, 1867, 1871, 1876, 1877, 1880 and 1886. She always insisted that she was absorbed in 'other and higher duties', which left no time or energy for public appearances. But how much work did Victoria actually do? There is no doubt that she was overwhelmed by the sheer volume of paperwork that confronted her after Albert's death. 'I must work and work, and can't rest and the amount of work which comes upon me is more than I can bear!'[29] Heaping insult upon injury, the prime minister, Palmerston, wrote to her four days after Albert died refusing her request for a private secretary.[30] The despatch boxes which arrived daily and piled up in her room certainly seemed to prove her claim that 'from the hour she gets out of bed until she gets into it again there is work work work'.[31]

Lord Clarendon, who was one of her more perceptive courtiers, considered that work kept the grieving queen sane: it compelled her to think of something other than her sorrow.[32] The government's refusal to allow her a private secretary was not as harsh as it seemed; the history of the office meant that an appointment would signal that the queen was incapable. General Grey, who had served Albert

as private secretary for twelve years, became her private
secretary in all but name. In 1868 the Tory government at
last agreed to give him official recognition. Victoria wrote
describing his duties in 1862:

General Grey do be so good as to let the Queen know
<u>whenever</u> he has any letters to show to her, and if she has
time She will see him, and if not he may send them up. But
he should let her know daily and in this same way be so
kind as to look through the newspapers and tell her what is
in them.[33]

This hardly suggests a workaholic monarch.

Victoria was conscientious, she did her signing and she
held occasional audiences. But she lacked the capacity for
statecraft to act as permanent minister in the way that
Albert had done. She took little interest in politics, and she
found 'those two dreadful old men' Palmerston and Russell
unbearable.[34] Political conversation was banned at the
queen's dinner table. Albert's 'secretariat' was dropped, and
his filing system abandoned. Unknown to the queen, her
German secretaries, who were in charge of filing, gave up
cross-referencing, and for the next four decades her papers
were stuffed into a cupboard. Revealingly, she did not discover that this had been going on until 1900.[35] Her real
work, as she saw it, was to commemorate the beloved's
memory, composing memoirs, commissioning biographies,
building the mausoleum at Frogmore and supervising the
design of the Albert Memorial in South Kensington.

As her sorrow abated, her household noticed that her

grief remained a reason for not doing things she didn't want to do, especially appearing in public. 'Eliza is roaring well and can do everything she likes and nothing she doesn't,' said Clarendon in 1869.[36] (Eliza was the household's name for the queen – the Brenda of the day.) In fact, Eliza had badly miscalculated.

1. A new dawn: Victoria in her coronation year, 1838. Sully's painting captures her youthful confidence and innocence.

2. 'If one has a husband one worships [marriage] is a foretaste of heaven!' Winterhalter's 'secret' bedroom painting which Victoria gave to Albert on his twenty-fourth birthday.

3. Albert, painted by Sir William (Charles) Ross, at the time of his marriage, proudly displaying the Garter ribbon which Victoria gave him as a wedding present.

4. *The Royal Family in 1846*, by Winterhalter. Albert dominates this unreal scene in which the royal couple wear formal court dress while their children play.

5. 1861: the workaholic Albert looks older than his forty years.

6. Victoria in 1877. Von Angeli, an artist whom Victoria admired because he did not flatter, shows the fifty-eight-year-old matriarch, red-faced and masterful.

7. 'View from my window at Balmoral by moonlight, October 1864.' Victoria was an accomplished watercolour artist, but after Albert's death she very rarely painted people.

8. Landseer's 1867 painting of Victoria at Osborne seemed to suggest an improper relationship between the queen and her Highland Servant, John Brown.

9. This photograph of the queen's Indian servant Abdul Karim ('the Munshi') towering over Victoria in a domineering fashion as she worked caused an outcry (1897).

10. Golden Jubilee, 1887. Grandmama of Europe: the queen-empress (seated, centre) surrounded by fifty-four members of her family, by the Danish painter Laurits Tuxen.

11. Sketch by Laurits Tuxen. At seventy-five, Victoria still took an intense interest in everything around her.

7
Mrs Brown

Balmoral, June 1866. Victoria is alone with her Highland Servant, John Brown. Tall, well built and conspicuous in a kilt which shows off his whipcord-muscled legs, the forty-year-old Brown is the queen's favourite. He tells her: 'I wish to take care of my dear good mistress till I die. You'll never have an honester servant.' She then takes and holds his 'dear kind hand'. With this exchange, the relationship enters a new phase. Brown becomes something more than a servant – an intimate friend.

> Afterwards my beloved John would say: 'You haven't a more devoted servant than Brown' – and oh! how I felt that!
>
> Afterwards so often I told him that no one loved him more than I did or had a better friend than me: and he answered 'Nor you – than me'. 'No one loves you more.'[1]

The source for this touching scene is an undated letter written by the queen after John Brown's death to his brother Hugh, into which she copied an extract from 'an old Diary or Journal of mine'. The journal as rewritten by Princess Beatrice contains no reference to any of this – and without

Victoria's full account we will never really know how close the relationship was.*

John Brown, who had been the queen's favourite gillie at Balmoral, was summoned to Osborne to lead her pony in 1864. The idea originated with Princess Alice, who thought Brown would help to relieve the queen's grief. Promoted to the post of the queen's Highland Servant in 1865, he took orders from the queen, came to her room after breakfast and after luncheon, and was constantly in attendance, both indoors and out. She drew strength from the simple, direct words of this 'faithful friend'. Worried that her grief for Albert had become less acute, compromising her loyalty to her beloved, she sought guidance from the Dean of Windsor. He assured her that Brown was sent by God to comfort her.[2]

Already there was gossip. The household joked that she was 'Mrs Brown', and her daughters referred to Brown as 'Mama's lover'.[3] The *Lausanne Gazette* printed a story in September 1866 that Victoria had secretly married Brown and was pregnant with his child. Observers noted that Victoria was putting on weight and had become red in the face, but the claim that she gave birth at the age of forty-seven was a libel. The story has reappeared in various versions ever since – the most recent account was published in 2012.[4] Tales of illegitimate births are an occupational hazard of royal biography, and the fact that John Brown

---

* Three hundred letters from Queen Victoria relating to John Brown were destroyed by Edward VII.

was Victoria's only alleged lover means that scurrilous gossip clusters thickly around him.

The relationship between Queen Victoria and John Brown was improper nonetheless. The queen seemed determined to flaunt her affection for her Highland Servant. As the Conservative politician Lord Stanley (later Derby) wrote in his diary in 1866:

> She is really doing all in her power to create suspicions which I am persuaded have no foundation. Long solitary rides, in secluded parts of the park: constant attendance upon her in her room: private messages sent to him by persons of rank: avoidance of observation while he is leading her pony or driving her little carriage: everything shows that she has selected this man for a kind of friendship which is absurd and unbecoming her position.[5]

The fact that Brown was a rough, uneducated Highlander made his proximity to the queen a scandal. Power in a court is a matter of gaining access to the monarch, and Brown, who saw her more than anyone, used his influence to block others – especially her children – from speaking to her. Lords-in-waiting were shocked when Brown put his head round a door and bawled: 'All what's here dines with the Queen.'[6]

Balmoral was Brown's fiefdom. Victoria now spent more time there than before, travelling north in the spring as well as the autumn, escaping for four months a year to her remote Highland retreat. At the gillies' ball, the only social occasion which she enjoyed nowadays, she sat on a low dais in the tented ballroom, her beady eye fixed on the reelers – she was an expert dancer and knew all the steps – while Brown acted as master of ceremonies, roughly pushing around the guests. 'What a coarse animal that Brown is,' said the Lord Chancellor. 'I did not conceive it possible that anyone could behave so roughly as he does to the Queen.' Victoria, however, seemed unmoved, telling funny stories at dinner heedless of the crashing of plates dropped by inebriated servants in the corridors. Someone asked Brown whether he was bringing tea on a drive into the hills with the queen. '"Wall, no," he replied, "she don't much like tea. We tak oot biscuits and sperruts [spirits]".'[7]

Did the queen know of the gossip? If, as some thought, she was aware of it, her response was astounding in its artlessness. In 1866 she commissioned Landseer to paint her 'as I am now, sad and lonely, seated on my pony, led by Brown'.[8] Entitled *Her Majesty at Osborne, 1866*, this large canvas showed the queen in deepest mourning mounted on her black pony reading letters from her official red box. The pony is held by Brown, and the painting suggests a startling intimacy between the queen and her black-kilted Highland Servant. When it was exhibited at the Royal Academy in the summer of 1867, it provoked sniggers from the crowd and outraged comments from the press.

Such was the unpopularity of Brown that radicals hatched a plot to hoot him if he appeared on the box of the queen's carriage at a military review in Hyde Park in July 1867. The prime minister felt obliged to warn the queen and advise her to leave Brown behind, and she objected furiously; fortunately the review was cancelled. But, as Lord Stanley observed in his diary, if Brown really was the queen's lover, 'there would not be all this publicity'.[9] Victoria herself was '<u>deeply</u> annoyed', and dismissed the 'lies' about Brown as '<u>ill-natured</u> gossip in the higher classes'.[10]

Victoria hit back at her critics with a memoir: a volume of extracts from her diary entitled *Leaves from the Journal of our Life in the Highlands 1848–61* (1868). This revealed Victoria and Albert living a simple, outdoor life of picnics and expeditions into the hills. In the footnotes Victoria lavished praise on her Highland servants, singling out Brown in particular, and the editor claimed that the queen's concern for the welfare of her household testified to her ardent wish 'that there should be no abrupt severance of class, but rather a gradual blending together of all classes'.[11] Victoria was certainly close to her servants, and in her journals she wrote often of them, but Princess Beatrice later omitted many of the passages referring to them when she copied the journals. *Leaves* was an instant best-seller – 100,000 copies were sold within three months. Victoria herself believed that 'the publication of my book did me more good than anything else'.[12]

The gossip about Brown scarred her. She was more bitter than ever about fashionable Society, criticizing the aristocracy for their frivolity, love of pleasure, self-indulgence and idleness which, she declared, resembled the French nobility on the eve of the Revolution.[13] Protecting good, honest Brown from sharp-tongued socialites gave a moral justification for her seclusion.

Staying at Balmoral in 1869, the sculptor Boehm was certain (though he had no evidence) that 'actual sexual intercourse' took place between Victoria and the 'Queen's

Stallion', as Brown was known. According to the diarist Wilfrid Blunt, who wrote down Boehm's story: '[Brown] was rude to the Queen, but she submitted to it all, though he was often drunk and smoked in her presence, a thing utterly forbidden to everyone. She used to go away with him to a little house in the hills where, on the pretence that it was for protection and "to look after her dogs" he had a bedroom next to hers, the ladies in waiting being put at the other end of the building.'[14]

Lady Chatterley-type sexual infatuations of upper-class women with their gamekeepers tend to be short-lived. Brown was not good company; he was often drunk; he grew fat, and the queen was far more intelligent than him. Yet her affection showed no signs of wearing off. According to one report noted by Lewis Harcourt in his dairy, Norman McLeod, the minister at Balmoral, a man whose spiritual counsel the queen valued greatly, confessed on his deathbed in 1872 that he had performed a service of marriage.[15] In 1873 the queen took communion for the first time in the Presbyterian kirk at Crathie – a momentous step for the head of the Anglican Church – and after this she grew very close to Brown's family. Most of Victoria's letters to Brown have been destroyed, but a surviving note from 1874 addresses Brown as 'darling one'.[16] In 1877 Lord Stanley (now Derby), found Brown in 'more extraordinary favour than ever', spending two hours alone with the queen every day. A few months later, he heard that Brown slept in a room adjoining her bedroom, 'contrary to all etiquette and even decency', and that 'the belief in a private marriage is general among the household, though they are ashamed or afraid to talk of it'.[17]

Brown died suddenly in 1883 of the skin disease erysipelas. He was fifty-six. Victoria was bedridden at the time, having fallen downstairs and injured her knee a few days before. Brown had carried her to her room, lifting her and raising her dress in a fashion which her doctor, James Reid, thought unseemly.[18] After Brown's death Victoria lost the use of her legs altogether, and she was unable to walk for several months. The queen described herself as 'utterly crushed' – 'her life has again sustained one of those shocks like in 61 when every link has been shaken & torn'.[19] It was as if she was widowed once again. 'The Queen feels that life for the second time is becoming most trying and sad to bear deprived of all she so needs.'[20] She memorialized Brown with a life-size bronze statue at Balmoral, inscribed with words suggested by Tennyson: 'Friend more than Servant, Loyal, Truthful, Brave/Self less than Duty, even to the Grave.' (The inscription would have been equally appropriate on a dog's grave.) To the horror of her children and household, she threatened to publish a biography of Brown as she had done of Albert, but her advisers succeeded in persuading her to drop the project. Among the many items which she directed to be placed in her coffin was a 'plain gold wedding-ring which had belonged to the mother of my dear valued servant and friend Brown and was given him by her in '75 – which he wore for a short time and I have worn constantly since his death – to be on my fingers'.[21]

*

What are we to make of all this? John Brown was certainly more important to Victoria than most biographers have believed. The fact that Princess Margaret attempted to block the publication of Victoria's instructions about Brown's ring as late as 1987 suggests a royal cover-up.[22] The evidence which has emerged since the 1970s points to a relationship far closer than that of servant and mistress.*

Did they or didn't they sleep together? is the question that everyone asks. For Victoria's sake one rather hopes they did, and the opportunity certainly existed; but this would not have been in character, though there is evidence of physical closeness, especially of Brown lifting and holding the queen. Several sources suggest that Victoria felt the need for some sort of blessing or marriage service, which would give the friendship moral or religious validation or – less likely perhaps – legitimize a sexual relationship. What is abundantly clear is the queen's emotional dependence on Brown. She confided in him about everything, and he was 'the only person who could fight and make the Queen do what she did not wish'.[23] In this respect the relationship resembled a marriage. In some ways, it was healthier than her marriage to Albert. Brown did not undermine Victoria's confidence, he never infantilized her in the way that Albert did. Above all, he was the '<u>dearest</u> & <u>best</u> friend' of a lonely widow who 'for 18 years & a ½ <u>never</u> left me for a day'.[24]

---

* Wilfrid Blunt's sensational diary was embargoed until 1975. The papers of Victoria's doctor James Reid were published in 1987 and the Stanley/Derby diaries in 1978 and 1994. Lewis Harcourt's account of Norman McLeod's deathbed confession came out in 2006.

The question that needs to be asked is whether the emotional benefits were outweighed by the harm that the relationship did to her reputation. At issue here is the queen's judgement. True, the damage could have been much worse. Compare Rasputin, the favourite of Victoria's granddaughter the Tsarina Alexandra of Russia. Like Rasputin, Brown was a man from the extremity of the kingdom, and his rough manner and lack of respect for the etiquette of the court were part of his appeal. Like Rasputin, too, Brown rose through his ability to cure a royal ailment: he alleviated the queen's depression. By contrast with Rasputin, however, Brown's influence was confined largely to stables, shooting and servants, and he made no attempt to meddle in religion or politics. How much more dangerous it would have been if the queen's friend had been a politician or a German prince. But Brown was a bully and often drunk, and Victoria allowed him to disrupt the working of her court. Nor did she make any attempt to stop him coming between her and her children. With his death, the sixty-four-year-old queen was at last released from the problem of reconciling her position as sovereign with a relationship with a man, whether dead or alive – a problem she had never really resolved.

8
Dearest Mama

Osborne, February 1868. Queen Victoria sits beside the bed of her pale-faced fourteen-year-old son Leopold. Still very weak, he is recovering from a terrifying attack of haemorrhaging from the bowels. A week ago the queen stayed up with him all night, fearing that he would die. Leopold is a bleeder. His illness, haemophilia, is caused (says the queen) by 'the peculiar constitution of the blood vessels, which have no adhesiveness', and there is no cure.[*][1] She vows that 'henceforth this dear Child; who as it were has been given back to me from the brink of the grave must be my chief object in life'.[2]

As a mother, Victoria alternated between smothering and neglect. Anxious to prevent accidents which might cause bleeding, she overprotected and micromanaged Leopold. At the same time, she blindly entrusted him to the care of John Brown's surly brother Archie, whose job it was to carry him when he was too ill to walk. Leopold hated the 'dreadful Scotch servants' who bullied and abused him, 'hitting me on the face with spoons for fun etc'. Leopold's governor, the man in charge of his education, was an officer named

---

[*] See p.113 for haemophilia.

Walter Stirling, to whom he was greatly attached. When Stirling quarrelled with Archie Brown, Victoria, who refused to see any faults in her Highland servants, promptly sacked Stirling, leaving Leopold to the mercy of 'that <u>devil</u> Archie'. Leopold's ally was his older sister Louise, but the queen forbade her from spending time with him. 'Lucy I don't know what would happen to me if you ever went away, all would be over with me then,' wailed Leopold.[3]

Victoria believed that Leopold was the only one of her four sons who had inherited Albert's brains. Nevertheless, she was determined to keep him at home and block his ambition to go to Oxford. 'I think he is happier now because he sees where his course lies, and does not think of what he cannot have,' she wrote.[4] This was not Leopold's understanding of his situation. Battling illness, pain and depression, he ached to escape from his gilded prison. Victoria kept him under close surveillance. 'Every inch of liberty is taken away from one, and one is watched, and every thing one says or does is reported,' he complained. Spying on her children – surrounding them with doctors and servants charged to report back to her – allowed the queen to exercise control, though she spent little time with them. When eventually Victoria gave in and allowed Leopold to attend university, he was bombarded (he wrote) with 'bullying <u>letters</u> and <u>telegrams</u>' from "Home, <u>sweet</u> home"'.[5]

Victoria was sometimes a monster, especially towards her older children. 'The House of Hanover produce bad parents,' a royal librarian once remarked. 'They are like ducks, they trample on their young.'[6] Victoria had always adhered to what Albert termed the 'aggressive system' of parenting, and after Albert's death she trampled more than ever.

No one felt his mother's wrath more than the Prince of Wales. She criticized him mercilessly, badmouthing him to his sisters and complaining that he was 'totally, totally unfit' for 'ever becoming King'.[7] He was hastily married off to Princess Alexandra of Denmark, the bride whom Albert had chosen, and installed at Marlborough House and Sandringham, the remote Norfolk estate Albert had found for him. His role was to do the work Victoria refused to do: he must be 'social sovereign', presiding over London Society, while the reclusive queen attended to the real business of ruling.

Victoria's difficult relationship with Bertie was perhaps an atavistic throwback to her Hanoverian ancestors, who had made a habit of quarrelling with their eldest sons. Victoria saw her heir as a political threat, as had been the habit of the four Georges. By denying him access to state papers and refusing to allow him a public role, she condemned him to forty years of waiting. For the prince, social life became an end in itself. If anyone was to blame for Bertie's lack of preparation for becoming king it was Victoria. In spite of this – or perhaps because of it – he was an unexpectedly successful and effective monarch.

Shortly before his death Albert told Victoria: 'My advice to be less occupied with yourself and your own feelings is really the kindest I can give.'[8] Grief, as we have seen, made her more than ever self-absorbed. Her needs must always come before those of her children, and 'managing her or in the slightest degree contradicting her' had become almost impossible.[9] The younger children still at home were locked into a prison of gloom and black crêpe. Cheerfulness was crushed as disloyalty to Papa's memory.

Victoria exposed some of her children to more emotional stress than they could bear, possibly damaging them psychologically. The eighteen-year-old Alice nursed her dying father, spending hours alone with him at his bedside, and then acted as comforter to her hysterically grieving mother, enduring sleepless nights on a bed in Victoria's room. Thin and exhausted, she was scarred – perhaps for life – by her traumatic experiences, plagued by depression and doubt.[10] On the night that Albert died, Victoria snatched the sleeping four-year-old Beatrice and took her to her own bed; according to legend, she wrapped the child in the nightclothes of the dead Albert. Though this story is most probably apocryphal, it stands as a metaphor for Victoria's treatment of her youngest child and favourite daughter. Beatrice was always 'Baby', her mother's pet, comforter and slave; she must never leave home, never attain sexual maturity or marry as other girls did.[11]

Victoria clung to her daughters. She wrote in 1863: 'A married daughter I MUST have living with me, and must not be left constantly to look about for help, and to have to make shift for the day, which is too dreadful!'[12] The first daughter to fill this role was Alice. Alice's marriage to Prince Louis of Hesse-Darmstadt in the summer of 1862 was 'more like a funeral than a wedding', and afterwards Victoria tried to persuade her daughter to stay in Britain.[13] She had become dependent on Alice's help and company, and she felt that 'I <u>can</u> <u>say</u> <u>every</u> thing to <u>you</u>, as I can to <u>no</u> <u>one else</u>'.[14]

When Alice moved with her husband to Darmstadt, the role of helpmate was taken by the next daughter, Princess Helena (known as Lenchen). Unswervingly obedient and, as a girl, lacking in imagination or social ambition, Helena fitted the bill perfectly. Victoria managed to keep her close at hand by marrying her to a balding, cash-strapped, chain-smoking German princeling fifteen years her senior, Prince Christian of Schleswig-Holstein, on condition that he came to live at Windsor. Alice tried to interfere with this plan, making Victoria furious: 'When your parent and your sovereign settles a thing for her good which interferes with none of your rights and comforts, opposition for mere selfish and personal objects – indeed out of jealousy – is monstrous,' she stormed.[15] Alice, once the favourite, was plunged into disgrace.

After Helena's marriage, her place was filled by the fourth daughter, Louise. Instead of taking London Society by storm as she might have hoped, the beautiful Louise wore herself out copying family letters for her tyrannical mother. When Louise rejected the idea of marrying a German prince, Victoria pushed her into marrying a subject: Lord Lorne, the heir to the Duke of Argyll. This radical new departure annoyed Victoria's children, who disapproved of marriage to a commoner, and Victoria herself found it hard to adapt to having a British subject as a son-in-law. 'There are <u>little</u> things in <u>his</u> manner – like that of all the young Englishmen,' she wrote, 'which a little startle the Queen who has never been on familiar terms strange to say ... with <u>any</u> but for-eign' young princes.[16] Perhaps the truly startling thing was how foreign and out of touch Victoria herself had become.

Queen Victoria declared that, with Louise's marriage to Lorne, she had jettisoned Albert's dynastic project altogether. 'Times have changed,' she wrote. 'Great foreign alliances are looked on as causes of trouble and anxiety and are of no good.' Not only were parliamentary grants to German 'beggars' unpopular in Britain, but the dynastic marriages of Vicky and Bertie to the royal families of Prussia and Den-mark had caused a painful rift within the family when Prussia invaded Denmark in 1864.[17] Louise, however, was the only one of Victoria's children to marry a commoner. Though Victoria no longer planned grand alliances for her younger children, the marriages were dynastic nonetheless. There was a dynastic intention behind Helena's marriage – though a poor relation, Prince Christian was the son of the Duke of Augustenburg, the unsuccessful claimant to the duchies of Schleswig and Holstein in 1864.*

Victoria claimed that she made no attempt to dictate her younger sons' choice of bride. 'My course is simply to say – there are these few unmarried Protestant Princesses – whom I hear generally well spoken of – choose for yourself amongst them.'[18] This was hardly non-interference. Alfred

---

* Christian's older brother, who became Duke of Augustenburg, was married to the daughter of Victoria's sister Feodore. With Helena's marriage to Prince Christian, Victoria signalled her opposition to Den-mark's claims to the duchies of Schleswig and Holstein, thus deepening the rift with the pro-Danish Alix and Bertie.

Duke of Edinburgh rejected the Protestant princesses produced by his mother in favour of Marie, daughter of Tsar Alexander II. This was not a great alliance but 'an apolitical dynastic curiosity'.[19] Leopold, the most rebellious of Victoria's sons, was instructed by his mother to meet Princess Helen of Waldeck and Pyrmont, and – uncharacteristically obedient – fell genuinely in love. 'It was entirely my own idea,' crowed Victoria.[20] It was also an idea entirely compatible with her strategy of allying with minor German princes. Arthur, Duke of Connaught, the queen's favourite son, anticipated the wishes of his beloved Mama by finding a suitable German princess all by himself – Princess Louise Margaret of Prussia.

After Louise's marriage, her place as amanuensis was taken by the sixteen-year-old Beatrice. 'She is my constant companion,' wrote the queen of her daughter, 'and I hope and trust will never leave me while I live.'[21] Trapped in her mother's dull court, Beatrice the spoilt little girl grew up to become a placid, lethargic and rather overweight young woman. When, aged twenty-seven, she fell unexpectedly in love with Prince Henry Battenberg, Victoria was beside herself with rage. For seven months she refused to talk to her daughter, enduring silent meals and communicating by notes. Eventually she gave way but only on condition that the prince abandoned his army career and came to live at the English court.

Victoria's two submissive daughters, Helena and Beatrice, remained on call for life. When she grew old they closed in, dealing with her correspondence, taking dictation of her letters and journal, and forming a 'harem' which caused the other siblings to feel excluded and resentful.

Vicky, Alice and Louise, on the other hand, escaped their mother's control through marriage. All three were independent-minded, successful women (and tremendous talkers). As such, both Louise and Vicky earned their mother's respect (Alice died of diphtheria aged thirty-five in 1878, before the rift with Victoria was healed). Victoria was Vicky's closest ally in her troubled life in Germany; and Victoria did her best to ease the pain of Louise's unhappy and childless marriage to Lorne. But there remained a difference of outlook between mother and daughters, and it was articulated in terms of attitudes towards the position of women. Vicky, Alice and Louise all sympathized with the women's movement. The queen, who never shed her burka-like black widow's mourning, was, by contrast, horrified at 'the mad, wicked folly of "women's rights"'. 'It is a subject', wrote Victoria, who was herself probably the most powerful woman in the world, 'which makes the Queen so furious that she cannot contain herself.'[22]

9
The Faery:
Gladstone and Disraeli

Balmoral, 26 September 1871. Prime Minister William Gladstone arrives as minister in attendance. Gladstone is sixty-two, but he looks younger. His figure is trim and his hair still black; the lines etched deep into his granite face show stern determination. He is on a mission to reform the monarchy and force the queen to attend to her public duties. Victoria is recuperating from a serious illness, with an abscess under her arm and 'flying' rheumatic pains. She refuses to see him and communicates from her dark-green tartan bedroom by writing notes which are delivered by a footman. Gladstone goes for long walks in the rain, and talks unceasingly about the Royalty Question, by which he means the retirement of the queen and the scandalous behaviour of the Prince of Wales. Not until six days later, on 1 October, does the queen feel well enough for a brief interview. Gladstone finds her much thinner – she has lost two stone. Faced by what he calls her 'repellent power', he realizes he is now 'on a new and different footing with her'.[1] Sovereign and minister are on the brink of war.

The quarrel started in August, when Gladstone tried to persuade the queen to delay her departure to Balmoral by a few days until the end of the parliamentary session. This modest request provoked an outburst of histrionics. 'What killed her beloved Husband?' raged the queen. 'Overwork and worry ... and the Queen, a woman, no longer young [she was fifty-two] is ... to be driven and abused till her nerves & health will give way.'[2] Gladstone by now had had enough of the royal malingering. 'Worse things may easily be imagined,' he wrote, 'but smaller and meaner cause for the decay of Thrones cannot be conceived. It is like the worm which bores the bark of a noble oak tree and so breaks the channel of its life.'[3]

Two years earlier, General Grey, Victoria's private secretary, had become so exasperated by her wilfulness that he wrote to Gladstone, advising him to discount her stories of shattered nerves and overwork: the queen, said Grey, was 'wonderfully well' and did very little work.[4] This was an act of startling disloyalty for a royal adviser, and it reveals the extent of Grey's desperation. When he confronted the queen about her refusal to appear in public, she dismissed him as an irritable old man and, complaining that he was impossible to work with, she avoided him.[5]

Victoria's children also defected. All of them (except Beatrice) signed a letter drafted by Vicky, imploring 'our adored Mama and our Sovereign' to take notice of 'the state of public feeling, which appears to us so very alarming'.[6] But no one dared speak out. The children's letter was not sent. Gladstone left Balmoral cheated of a confrontation by Victoria's illness which, this time at least, was real.

Critics complained that the queen failed to give the taxpayer value for money. *What Does She Do With It?* shrieked a radical pamphlet, which accused the invisible queen of hoarding from the civil list. When in 1871 the queen requested parliamentary grants for two of her children – for Louise on her marriage, and for Arthur on his coming of age – it seemed that she was being outrageously greedy. The attacks were not altogether fair. The queen received a civil list or annual grant from Parliament of £385,000 (£17.6 million in today's money), and she made savings from this sum which enabled her to amass a large personal fortune. The savings were not due to her retirement, however, as her opponents claimed, but to the cuts which Prince Albert had effected when he reorganized the household in the 1840s.*[7] What made Victoria's finances a political issue was the rise of a republican movement, inspired by the Commune in Paris and led by the radical MP Charles Dilke, who launched his campaign with a speech at Newcastle in November.

The republican movement was snuffed out almost immediately by the dangerous illness of the Prince of Wales. The drama of Bertie's near-death from typhoid on the same day in 1871 – 14 December – that Albert had died ten years before electrified the nation. The surge of sympathy for the queen and prince revealed, as the journalist Walter Bagehot noted, the shallowness of republicanism and the depth of personal loyalty which underpinned the monarchy.[8]

---

* Over the course of her reign Victoria saved an estimated £800,000 (£36.5 million in 2005 prices) from the civil list, which went into the Privy Purse. She agreed to pay income tax in 1842.

Bertie's recovery offered Gladstone an opportunity that he was quick to seize. He insisted that the queen and her son should attend a public thanksgiving at St Paul's Cathedral. Victoria reluctantly agreed, though she found the 'religious part' to be 'MOST distasteful to her feelings'.[9] For Gladstone, a religious ceremony gave expression to his sacramental view of monarchy as ordained by God. As so often with Gladstone, high principle sat uneasily beside political calculation. A public demonstration of support for the throne would effectively extinguish the republican movement, which threatened to upset the precarious alliance of Whig grandees and radicals within Gladstone's Liberal Party.

In spite of Victoria's misgivings and grumbling, and regardless of her refusal to process in the state carriage and her dislike of St Paul's ('so dull, cold, dreary, and dingy'), the thanksgiving on 27 February 1872 was a resounding success. Even Victoria was moved by the cheering of the densely packed London crowds: 'It was a most affecting day, and many a time I repressed my tears.'[10] For this publicity coup, Victoria had Gladstone to thank. But though she expressed 'her warmest and most heartfelt thanks to the whole Nation for this great demonstration of loyalty', she showed little gratitude to her prime minister.[11] Nor was she at all amused by his follow-up proposal: to give employment to the Prince of Wales by appointing him Viceroy of Ireland.

Gladstone chose to communicate his plan to the queen as if she were a public department, by composing a densely argued thirty-four-page letter. This Victoria read with 'a good deal of irritation'. Her private opinion was that preparation of the Prince of Wales for becoming king was 'quite useless'.[12] She wrote a discouraging reply, implying that sending the prince to Ireland risked entangling the crown with Gladstone's controversial Irish policy. Gladstone refused to take the hint. Instead he bombarded her with long and argumentative memoranda. Only when Victoria told him plainly that it was 'useless' to prolong discussion did Gladstone drop the matter.[13] By then he and Victoria had become estranged.

Who was chiefly at fault – Victoria or Gladstone – for this falling-out is debatable. Victoria was not especially partisan in 1868 when Gladstone became prime minister. Nor was she ill-disposed towards him. As a protégé of Robert Peel, Gladstone had been talent-spotted by Albert, who liked him, and while Albert was alive he was on friendly terms with the queen. As one of Gladstone's biographers perceived, the question that needs to be asked is: how was it that Gladstone allowed the rift to come about?[14]

When Gladstone took office in 1868, the Dean of Windsor, Gerald Wellesley, advised him that the queen was far more nervous than formerly, and she needed to be managed with gentleness, even tenderness. 'Where you differ it will be best not at first to try and reason her over to your side but pass the matter lightly over with expression of respectful regret, and reserve it.'[15] This advice was followed to the letter by Disraeli, but Gladstone chose to ignore it.

The irony was that Gladstone's intentions were benign. A devoted monarchist, he understood that the new political order created by the 1867 franchise extension had transformed the role of the sovereign, which 'may chiefly be perceived in the beneficial substitution of influence for power'.[16] Hence his insistence on more public appearances by the queen. But his overbearing, confrontational manner made Victoria feel inadequate; her distrust of his growing radicalism fuelled her dislike, and she came to consider him 'dangerous': 'so very arrogant, tyrannical and obstinate, with no knowledge of the world or human nature', and 'a fanatic in religion'.[17]

Henry Ponsonby, whom Victoria appointed as her private secretary in 1870, played a crucial part in containing the conflict with Gladstone. Shrewd, untidily dressed and drily amused, he was not a typical courtier. Most of the household were Tories, but he was a Liberal and made no attempt to hide it. Unlike Grey – or Gladstone – Ponsonby never confronted Victoria on the subject of her seclusion. He knew that to do this was to risk losing his influence with her, and then his position would be untenable, as Grey's had been. He never contradicted her; he knew she could not admit that she was wrong. 'When she insists that 2 and 2 make 5 I say that I cannot help thinking they make 4. She replies there may be some truth in what I say, but she knows they make 5. Thereupon I drop the discussion.'[18] In writing the queen's political letters to Gladstone, Ponsonby acted as translator, extracting the gist of her meaning and silently filtering her violent opinions.

'He can only offer devotion.'[19]

With these words Disraeli accepted the queen's commission to lead a Tory minority government in February 1868.

The following day, the sixty-three-year-old prime minister arrived at Osborne. 'You must kiss hands,' said Victoria as she came into her closet, holding out her hand.[20] Disraeli fell to his knees and took Victoria's plump hand in his, and as he kissed it, he said, 'in loving loyalty and faith'.[21] Then the queen sat down, which she only did in audiences with her prime minister, and talked of 'affairs' for half an hour while Disraeli remained standing.

Victoria thought her new minister 'a man "risen from the people"' (this was a strange way to describe a dandy Jewish novelist, but he was an outsider to the political classes) and she found him 'very peculiar'.[22] With his dyed black ringlets, his cadaverous face and the rings that he wore over his gloves, Disraeli was certainly that. When he destroyed Peel over the Corn Laws in 1846, Victoria had loathed 'that dreadful Disraeli', but now she found him 'full of poetry, romance and chivalry'; emotional intelligence was one of his strengths. Within days he was penning elegant, witty, confiding letters, seemingly admitting her to the inner circle of government. Victoria declared that she had never had such letters in her life – 'she never before knew <u>everything</u>'.[23] Disraeli made her feel, as only Melbourne had done, that he was *her* minister and devoted servant, and together she and he ruled the country.

Disraeli's first minority government lasted only ten months. On his return to office in 1874, he kissed hands and declared (Victoria wrote), '"I plight my troth to the kindest of <u>Mistresses</u>"!'[24] Both he and the queen had changed. Disraeli's eccentric but adoring wife, Mary Anne, had died; and Victoria's relations with Gladstone had almost reached breaking point. Ever the novelist, Disraeli composed a journal of his premiership or rather an epistolary novel, often bearing little relation to fact, in the romantic letters he wrote to two middle-aged married sisters, Lady Bradford and Lady Chesterfield.

In August 1874 Disraeli stayed at Osborne with the queen. 'I can only describe my reception by telling you that I really thought she was going to embrace me,' he wrote. 'She was wreathed with smiles, and as she tattled, glided about the room like a bird.' As a special mark of favour, defying the etiquette which dictated that the minister should stand, she offered him a chair. Disraeli thought it best to decline, but a triumphant letter to Lady Bradford flew from his pen. At Balmoral the following month Disraeli was ill and confined to his room. He wrote to Lady Bradford in high glee: 'This morning the Queen paid me a visit in my bedchamber. What do you think of that?'[25]

'I must say that I feel fortunate in having a female Sovereign,' Disraeli told Lady Bradford. 'I owe everything to woman.' He understood, as Gladstone did not, that confronting the queen would never succeed. 'I never deny,' he once explained, 'I never contradict; I sometimes forget.' He laid on the flattery, as he later said, 'with a trowel'; but the oil was salted with irony and a mocking self-awareness.[26] He perceived – as his biographer wrote – that the queen craved the friendship of someone who could cut through the layers of formal protocol which constituted her defence against familiarity or impertinence. In this he was not entirely dissimilar to John Brown.[27]

As a man who made hypochondria an art form, Disraeli

could sympathize when Victoria bemoaned her shattered health. Disraeli's sympathy was often expressed with his tongue in his cheek, but (as Ponsonby observed) 'are not her woes told in the same manner?'.[28] A lonely, childless widower with few friends and no family life, Disraeli perhaps understood that Victoria's self-imposed seclusion had locked her into a palace which had become a prison.

Disraeli played an elaborate game of courtly love with the queen. Thanking her for a gift of snowdrops from Osborne, he told her that he had placed them on his heart, and later, as he lay in bed, wondered whether they were a 'faery gift' which came from Queen Titania, Shakespeare's queen of the fairies, 'gathering flowers, with her Court, in a soft and sea-girt isle'.[29] Ponsonby dismissed Disraeli's letters as froth: 'it seems to me that he communicates nothing except boundless professions of love and loyalty and if called on to write more says he is ill'.[30] But Disraeli's hyperbole had a subtly mocking subtext. Anyone less like Titania than Queen Victoria would be hard to imagine. The queen did not know it, but Disraeli's nickname for her was the Faery. Nor was Disraeli blinded by devotion. At the time of the Titania letter he complained to Lord Derby that the queen was in a 'strange excited state of mind'. Not mad, but 'very troublesome, very wilful and whimsical, like a spoilt child: not without sympathy for others, but totally without consideration for their feelings or wishes'.[31] It was a shrewd insight.

Managing the spoilt-child queen – flattering and humouring her – was almost a full-time job; Disraeli was very good at it, but it took up a great deal of his time. This was time well spent, however. Disraeli was an ideologist of monarchy, and one of the first to perceive the new importance of the crown in riveting popular loyalties post-1867. Forging a bond between the queen and the Tory Party was sharp politics. Victoria rewarded Disraeli by opening Parliament on three occasions, in 1876, 1877 and 1880. The danger, as Derby warned, was that Disraeli's success risked 'encouraging in her too large ideas of her personal power'.[32]

One result of Disraeli's chumminess with the queen was the 1876 Royal Titles Act, creating her Empress of India. This was Victoria's idea. By yielding to her demand, Disraeli incurred opposition from the Prince of Wales (who was not consulted) and the Liberal Party. No doubt Victoria was influenced by the fact that Vicky stood in line to become German empress, which would give the daughter precedence, and Victoria certainly relished signing herself as V. R. I. (Victoria Regina et Imperatrix). But the gaudy title was in fact a clever gesture: as she wrote, 'it suits oriental ideas', and it gave expression to her strong, though virtual, relationship with her Indian empire.[33]

As before over the Crimea, it was war that stirred Victoria to intervene. When Turkey ignited the Eastern Crisis in the Balkans with a massacre of Bulgarian Christians in 1876, Gladstone emerged from retirement to set British politics alight. His pamphlet on *The Bulgarian Horrors and the Question of the East* castigated Disraeli's government for being complicit with the Turks.* Gladstone's campaign enraged the queen, who blamed the Russians for stirring up

---

* Victoria created Disraeli Earl of Beaconsfield in 1876, shortly before Gladstone's intervention in the Eastern Crisis.

trouble in the Balkans and considered that Gladstone's mischief-making had inflamed them. When Russia declared war against Turkey, her fury knew no limits. She saw things in simple, personalized terms, totally lacking in nuance – Queen of England versus the Tsar of Russia. 'Oh, if the Queen were a man, she would like to go and give those Russians . . . such a beating!' she wrote.[34] If anything made her blood boil more than the Russians, it was the madman Gladstone's unpatriotic barnstorming speeches. 'It is a miserable thing', she wrote, 'to be a constitutional Queen and to be unable to do what is right.'[35] 'The Faery writes every day and telegraphs every hour,' Disraeli groaned.[36] She bombarded the government with seventeen notes and telegrams in a single day. But if anyone was responsible for encouraging the Faery to play the role of warrior queen, it was Disraeli himself – her Grand Vizier, as he once playfully described himself.

Disraeli stands accused of blurring the lines between public and private, unscrupulously exploiting the personal affection of the queen in the interests of his party, as Melbourne had done before. He managed to correspond directly with the queen, so his letters escaped Ponsonby's filtering, as did hers. When the Tory government was defeated at the 1880 election, Victoria wrote asking him to drop the third person 'when we correspond – which I hope we shall on many a <u>private</u> subject and without anyone being astonished or offended, and even more without anyone knowing about it'.[37] We shall never know what she confided in Dizzy. After her death, Edward VII requested that Disraeli's executors return her private letters, and he ordered several packets to be destroyed.

Victoria was in Germany at the time of the 1880 election. 'I shall be glad to be away,' she wrote of the election, which she confidently expected Disraeli to win. To her horrified surprise, a 'calamity' occurred: Disraeli lost.[38]

Victoria returned to Windsor determined on one thing: Gladstone must not become prime minister. 'She will sooner <u>abdicate</u>,' she wrote, 'than send for . . . <u>that half-mad fire-brand</u> who wd soon ruin everything and be a <u>Dictator</u>.'[39] She claimed to be unable to give Gladstone her confidence because of his violent, mischievous and dangerous conduct in opposition. There must be '<u>no lowering</u> of the <u>high position</u> this country holds,' she wrote.[40] This stern language came closer to the words of Margaret Thatcher than the vocabulary of public duty used by the Windsors in the twentieth century. It was as if the queen were a headmistress, ticking off Gladstone for bringing the country into disrepute.

Disraeli, who advised throughout, cynically flouting constitutional convention, recommended her to send for the Whig leader, Lord Hartington (later Duke of Devonshire). This was correct, but politically unwise. It was true that Gladstone had resigned as leader of the opposition in 1875; but he had led the Liberal Party to victory with his Midlothian campaign over the Bulgarian Horrors and this made him impossible to resist as prime minister.

In the new era of two-party politics, however, the queen's

power of choosing – as opposed to formally appointing – the prime minister had melted away. Hartington told the queen that he was unable to form a government unless Gladstone agreed to serve. Gladstone refused to serve under anyone. Victoria had no option but to summon Gladstone, who kissed hands for the second time. The queen (according to Gladstone) behaved with 'perfect courtesy'. She told him frankly that she disliked the strong language that he had used in his speeches.[41] Later, she confided in Disraeli that Gladstone looked 'very ill, very old and haggard and his voice feeble'.[42]

Thus began Act Three of the drama of Victoria and her prime ministers. Gladstone at seventy had become an old man. His hair was white and wispy, his clothes disorderly, his eyes wild. 'To me,' wrote Victoria, '"the people's William" is a most disagreeable person – half crazy, and so excited.'[43] Protected by an adoring family and shielded by fawning private secretaries, the Grand Old Man was not used to being contradicted. He observed 'a serious and unhappy change' in the queen's manner.[44] She was more hostile and difficult than ever. He blamed Disraeli.

Between 1880 and 1885 Victoria sent Gladstone an estimated 207 letters and 170 telegrams, and Gladstone wrote her 1,107 letters. She peppered him with bossy, nagging messages to which he replied with long-winded letters laboriously putting her right. At audiences where, unlike Disraeli, he was never invited to sit, Gladstone felt he was always 'outside an iron ring, and, without any desire, had I the power to, break it through'. 'The Queen alone is enough to kill any man,' he groaned, consoling himself with the thought that she was jealous of his popularity.[45]

Especially after Disraeli died in 1881, Victoria felt out of touch. She complained that she had 'no one real independent friend' in the Cabinet, and that Gladstone told her nothing.[46] In her journal on New Year's Day 1881 she confessed that her temper was uncontrollable, but 'I am so overdone, so vexed, and in such distress about my country, that that must be my excuse'.[47] When at length Gladstone resigned in 1885, Victoria offered him an earldom, but Gladstone refused to accept political extinction. In 1892, when he became prime minister for the fourth time, Victoria found the Grand Old Man aged eighty-two 'a very alarming look-out': 'his face shrunk, deadly pale with a weird look in his eyes, a feeble expression about the mouth, and the voice altered'.[48]

In 1867 the *Economist* editor Walter Bagehot published a famous book on *The English Constitution* in which he drew a distinction between the decorative and efficient parts of the constitution. The queen no longer exercised executive power, said Bagehot, but the importance of her ceremonial, public role, in attracting public loyalty and giving government legitimacy, was incalculable. This was not how Victoria understood her position at all. She appeared in public reluctantly and only very occasionally, but she interfered constantly with her prime ministers. Nor did she follow Albert's example. Tearing up his rule about keeping out of party politics, she was shamelessly Tory.

How did she get away with it? Ponsonby helped, by pruning her letters and steering her away from a showdown with Gladstone. She owed a debt to Gladstone himself, who remained staunchly loyal; it never occurred to him to publicize the queen's persecution. On the contrary, he likened himself to a Sicilian mule he had once ridden – a beast of burden, for whom he had absolutely no feelings.[49] (Actually Victoria disliked him far more than any mule.) In the last analysis, Victoria's partisanship and meddling no longer mattered. Though she was slow to grasp the fact, her prerogative had shrunk so much that she could do little damage.[50]

10
Grandmama V. R. I.

In her sixties, Victoria changed. Like her great-great-granddaughter Elizabeth II, who also seemed stiff and out of touch in middle age (though much less so), Victoria softened. These are the years when she supposedly uttered the famous snub, 'We are not amused'. Whether or not the saying is apocryphal – and humour was not her strong point – it defines only one side of her personality.[1] Other people who came close reported her telling funny stories and laughing heartily until she was red in the face and tears ran down her cheeks – something that would have been unthinkable in her thirties or forties. Marie Mallet, her maid of honour, whose letters give the best account of these years, describes a warm-hearted, lively queen who seems a different person from the severe, grieving widow. Mallet noticed, however, that the queen took a morbid interest in deaths and funerals.[2] Lady Lytton, a lady-in-waiting, told Lytton Strachey that she 'adored the Queen. What she liked so much about her ... was the intense interest she took in every detail of the lives of everyone who was about her – "even the housemaids".'[3]

Courtiers claimed that the late-Victorian monarchy was the simplest court in Europe; it was also perhaps the most bizarre. The queen, immured in her private apartments, was rarely seen – indeed, the ritual of her court was constructed to hide her from view. All communication between H. M. and the household was by writing. Letters must be addressed simply 'The Queen', and the envelope secured with an official seal, not licked. The queen, who walked with a stick after she injured her knee in 1883, took a drive every afternoon, when she disliked meeting anyone. Members of the household who had the misfortune to encounter her carriage had to hide behind a bush.[4]

Dinner with the queen could be an ordeal. The simple meal – soup, fish, cold beef and the cream puddings of which Victoria was particularly fond – began at 9 and usually lasted precisely thirty minutes. The queen was served first and gobbled her food. Slow eaters such as Gladstone, who was said to chew each mouthful thirty-three times, found their plates snatched away by the servants when they had barely begun. Conversation was hushed and depended entirely on the queen's mood – sometimes she barely uttered a word. After dinner at Windsor the queen often sat in the corridor – guests wondered 'why, with all the rooms the Castle possessed, we should be confined to this small passage'.[5] People were brought up to her one by one for a brief and terrifying audience. At 11 she retired, and the gentlemen hastened to a distant room where the queen's smoking ban was relaxed. (All her family were enthusiastic smokers.) Shortly before midnight, one of her ladies was summoned to her sitting room to talk, read and take orders until 12.45 or later.

At Windsor, people talked in whispers as they walked

down the hushed, soft-carpeted corridors which led to the queen's private apartments. 'One door after another opened noiselessly, it was like passing through the forecourts of a temple, before approaching the final mystery to which only the initiated had access.'[6] The queen's private sitting room smelled of orange water, and it was hung high with portraits of her relations, cluttered with potted palms and screens and crowded with photographs and effigies of dead dogs. Here sat the queen with her dogs at her feet: an unbelievably small figure with a shy, sweet smile.

After the death of John Brown, Randall Davidson, Dean of Windsor, who had managed to dissuade the queen from publishing her life of Brown, wrote in his unpublished diary: 'There is a good deal more difficulty in dealing with a spoilt child of sixty or seventy than with a spoilt child of six or seven.' The queen, he thought, was one of those unfortunate people 'who had the extreme disadvantage all their life of being free from the unwholesome influence of their equals'.[7] Soon, however, the spoilt child was to become a wise and lovable old matriarch.

One sign of the change in Victoria was her discovery of the South of France. While in mourning for Albert in the 1860s, she had visited Coburg three times, but these trips were emotionally gruelling pilgrimages to the birthplace of the beloved. Her visits to the French Riviera were different. She first went there aged sixty-two in 1882, fleeing the gloom, rain and seclusion of her habitual spring at Balmoral. Travelling incognito as Countess of Balmoral (though her luggage was labelled Queen of England) in a special silk-hung train with a top speed of 35 m.p.h., sustained by Irish stew from Windsor kept warm in red flannels, she arrived beaming, less tired than anyone by the journey. John Brown, who hated 'abroad', made no attempt to conceal his grumpiness. Her suite sweated in their thick black dresses, but the queen thrived on the vitamin D and found the sun had 'a very invigorating, exhilarating effect on mind and body'. Liberated by Brown's death in 1883, she visited the Riviera a total of nine times, often staying as long as six weeks and enjoying everything 'as if she was 17 instead of 72'.[8]

From the mid 1880s, the Widow of Windsor was immune from political criticism. She was hailed as Britain's first constitutional monarch, a paragon of fairness and political impartiality.[9] Of course, this was a fiction. She was staunchly Tory, and determined above all to rid herself of the madman Gladstone. From 1885 she found in Lord Salisbury a Tory minister with whom she could do business. Unlike Disraeli, Salisbury was an insider, but he too was a political exotic. An immense, clumsy figure, cerebral and depressive, Salisbury was an unlikely leader of Britain's burgeoning democracy. Like Bismarck, he was a reactionary diplomatist resolved to preserve the aristocratic order; but he was a committed Christian with none of Bismarck's venom or dirty tricks.

'He feels so much for me and my being so alone, so cut off,' wrote the queen.[10] In 1886 Gladstone formed his third government, pledged to introduce Home Rule for Ireland, and Victoria conspired with Salisbury to engineer Gladstone's fall. Flouting the constitutional convention which forbade the monarch from corresponding with the leader of the opposition, Victoria cheerfully leaked Gladstone's letters to Salisbury.[11]

Salisbury was the first of Victoria's prime ministers to be younger than her but, like Disraeli, he was granted special privileges. On account of his weight – his legs could barely support his gigantic body – he was allowed to sit in her presence. At Balmoral, which Salisbury disliked, referring to it as Siberia, his rooms were specially heated to a temperature of 60 degrees. When she stayed near Nice, the queen often called on her prime minister, who owned a house nearby. 'I never saw two people get on better,' wrote Salisbury's daughter-in-law, 'their polished manners and deference to and esteem for each other were a delightful sight.'[12]

When his government was defeated in the 1892 election, Victoria bemoaned the 'defect in our much famed Constitution' which forced her 'to part with an admirable Govt like Ld Salisbury's for no question of any importance, or any particular reason, merely on account of the number of votes'.[13] As for Salisbury, he 'grew fonder of the Queen than of anyone outside his immediate family'. The architect of so-called 'Villa Toryism', he respected his mistress's judgement, writing that 'when I knew what the Queen thought, I knew pretty certainly what view her subjects would take, and especially the middle class of her subjects.'[14]

Victoria's Golden Jubilee, 21 June 1887. At 11.30 a.m. the queen's open carriage leaves Buckingham Palace, preceded by a long procession of royalties. Her face, notices one reporter, is 'not altogether free from apprehension', and with reason, as the sea of people lining the route seems unduly silent. But when her famous cream-coloured horses come into sight, the queen is greeted by a pent-up, deafening roar – a 'rich and tumultuous chorus of loyalty and affection'. This spontaneous outburst is as unexpected as it is moving. *The Times* notices that the tiny black figure is 'almost overcome', bowing right and left to the cheering crowd as the procession crawls towards Westminster Abbey.[15]

The pomp and pageantry of the Jubilee marked a new style, anticipating the ceremonial monarchy of the twentieth century, where public splendour and ritual took the place of real political power.[16] The presence in the procession of Indian princes and the Queen of Hawaii hinted at a new imperial relationship, riveting the crown to her subjects overseas. Loyalty to the queen-empress would become a membrane binding to London the far-flung parts of the map that were painted red.[17]

The Jubilee ceremony inside Westminster Abbey, however, evoked a much older idea of kingship. During the service, Victoria sat in the Coronation Chair '<u>alone</u>', just as she had been fifty years ago on the day of her accession. One by one, her sons and her grandsons 'stepped forward, bowed, and in succession kissed my hand, I kissing each'. Next came her daughters and granddaughters, who curtsied, and 'I embraced them warmly'.[18]

Gladstone, seated in the abbey, thought the service 'too courtly'.[19] But that was how Victoria meant it to be – and she had paid most of the bill out of her Privy Purse.* The act of homage masquerading as affection dramatized her position as head of this great family: as Grandmama V. R. I., which was how she signed herself in letters to her grandchildren. In the painting by the Danish artist Laurits Tuxen which Victoria commissioned to commemorate the Jubilee, the queen sits in the foreground, wearing her black evening dress and blue Garter ribbon, surrounded by fifty-four members of her family. Leopold's widow, the Duchess of Albany, kneels before Victoria with her baby son and daughter in a pose that suggests family feeling with a subtext of homage to the queen-empress.

Victoria's family of nine children and forty-two grandchildren had become a dynasty. They formed an imagined community – a dynastic realm, floating above and transverse to the nation-state, created and sustained by her.[20] In true dynastic style, the queen-empress had no surname that might tie her down to a national identity – her subjects knew her simply as Victoria.† Her grandchildren sat on the thrones of Germany, Russia, Spain, Norway, Romania, Greece and Sweden. Though German by descent, English was their common language and, in an age of growing

---

* The queen paid £50,000 (roughly £3 million in today's values) and the government £16,000 towards the Jubilee.
† When someone asked what her surname was, she replied, after some reflection, Guelph d'Este of the House of Brunswick. This was the Hanoverian surname; interestingly, she didn't mention Albert's names of Wettin or Saxe-Coburg-Gotha (*Life with Queen Victoria: Marie Mallet's Letters from Court 1887–1901*, ed. Victor Mallet, p. 150).

official nationalism, they were cosmopolitan, identifying more with the wider royal family than they did with their own people.

Acknowledged as head of the family since the death of her uncle Leopold in 1865, Victoria took her role seriously. As she told Vicky in 1876:

> The very large family with their increasing families and interests is an immense difficulty and I must add burthen for me. Without a husband and father, the labour of satisfying all (which is impossible) and of being just and fair and kind – and yet keeping often quiet which is what I require so much – is quite fearful.[21]

How did she do it? From the seclusion of her court, she penned a flood of letters, illegible but forthright, bombarding her family with advice and instructions. 'Never make friendships,' the queen told her granddaughters. Friendships with (non-royal) girls were 'very bad and often lead to great mischief': royals must hang together.[22]

They must marry one another too. Matchmaking was one of the queen's chief preoccupations, though she pretended to have nothing to do with it. She warned her granddaughters in Hesse not to get married 'for marrying's sake and to have a position . . . it is a very German view of things'. No longer did she push the claims of the Hohenzollerns, finding Vicky and Fritz 'not pleasant in Germany. They are high and mighty there.' She urged her German grandchildren to marry their English first cousins. More than anything she dreaded her Hesse granddaughters marrying

Russians. 'I have <u>such</u> a dislike to the fat Czar [Alexander III],' she wrote. 'I think him a violent, Paul-like Asiatic, full of hate, passion and tyranny.' When Alexandra of Hesse married Tsar Nicholas II of Russia, Victoria wrote, 'my blood runs cold when I think of her <u>so</u> young . . . on that vy. unsafe Throne'.[23]

Victoria has sometimes been blamed for ignoring medical advice about the risks of haemophilia in her matchmaking, especially over Alexandra's marriage to Nicholas II. Because of her haemophiliac son Leopold, who died aged thirty, Victoria was well aware of the illness, but she did not recognize that it was hereditary, nor that she herself was a carrier. Her daughter Alice's son Friederich was diagnosed as a bleeder and died aged two in 1873, and she wrote: 'This peculiarity of poor little Fritz, like Leopold's, which is such a rare thing and not in the family, is most extraordinary.'[24] Medical advice discouraged the marriage of bleeders and their sisters. But when Victoria consulted Sir William Jenner about the marriage of little Fritz's brother Ernest Duke of Hesse and his first cousin 'Ducky' (Victoria Melita) of Edinburgh, he replied: 'there was no danger and no objection as they are so strong and healthy . . . He said that if the relations were strong intermarriage between them only led to greater strength and health.'[25] Either the royal doctors did not understand the mechanisms of inheritance of X-linked chromosome disorders, or they did not dare tell the queen the facts.

With her grandchildren and great-grandchildren, there was real affection. 'Such was the majesty that surrounded Queen Victoria,' wrote the Duke of Windsor, 'that she was regarded almost as a divinity of whom even her own family stood in awe. However, to us children she was "Gangan"...'.[26] Beatrice's son 'Drino' (Lord Carisbrooke), who had lunch with his grandmother every day until the age of fourteen, claimed that 'the legend that nobody dared open their mouths is completely untrue'.[27] Vicky's daughter 'Moretta' (Princess Victoria of Prussia) described how, on the anniversary of her father's death, Grandmama 'was as sweet and touching as any mother could be. She took me in her arms, and kissed me over and over again.'[28]

She was especially close to the Hesse children after the death of their mother, Alice, in 1878. To her granddaughter Victoria of Hesse she wrote 'as a loving <u>Mother</u> (for I feel I <u>am that</u> to you beloved Children <u>far more</u> than a Grandmother).'[29] In 1885 the sixty-six-year-old queen-empress sat beside the bed of Victoria of Hesse, in childbirth, at Windsor from 7 a.m. until 5 p.m., when her first baby was born. The child, Alice Battenberg, was the future mother of Prince Philip. Few grandmothers insist on being present throughout their granddaughters' labour, but the queen found the experience 'strange, and indeed affecting'.[30]

As grandmother and matriarch and in her dynastic role, Victoria reached a way of reconciling the tensions between her gender and her rank. No longer was she tormented by the conflict between her roles as a woman – as a daughter, as a wife and mother – and her vocation as queen. She ceased to rail at the anomaly of being a woman on the throne. Nor did her widow's seclusion compromise her position as queen. At last, late in life, she had shaken off the constraints of marriage and the gloom of widowhood and found wisdom and fulfilment.

In the smudgy footage of the Diamond Jubilee (22 June 1897), the small, hunched figure of the seventy-eight-year-old monarch can be clearly seen, wearing black silk beneath a white parasol, seated in the state carriage, processing through a storm of acclamation.* By now she was too lame to dismount from her carriage, so the thanksgiving service was held on the steps of St Paul's Cathedral. 'Has one ever heard of such a thing!' tut-tutted her first cousin Augusta. 'After 60 years Reign to thank God in the Street!!!!'[31] But when the crowds gave a thunderous roar for the queen, tears ran down the old lady's face.

Her court was richly eccentric. Thrifty economies were practised, such as cutting newspapers into squares and recycling them as lavatory paper. At Windsor, Albert's blue room was still kept exactly as he had left it almost forty years before, and a servant still brought his hot water and laid out his evening clothes each night. ('Think of the mere waste of the servants' time!' commented Lady Lytton.)[32] And the queen was no less stubborn. Behind the show of the Diamond Jubilee there raged a furious row. The queen's Indian servant Abdul Karim, who had joined the household in 1887, was her acknowledged favourite. She appointed

---

* The footage is now on YouTube. Victoria saw it, and thought it 'very wonderful' but 'a little hazy and too rapid' (Elizabeth Longford, *Victoria* R. I., p. 549).

him her secretary (Munshi), took lessons from him in Hindustani, and even made him her Indian Secretary in spite of the fact that he was illiterate. The privileges and rewards that he extracted from the queen and his pretensions and influence caused deep resentment in the household. In 1897, when the Munshi was diagnosed with venereal disease, the household went on strike and threatened to boycott the queen's spring visit to the Riviera if he came too. There was a scene. In a terrifying (but robust) display of royal rage, Victoria swept all the objects on her desk onto the floor. The Munshi came to France, the suite came too, and the queen seemed blind to the trouble caused by her favouritism.

As her eyesight worsened, her handwriting, never legible, became impenetrable. Her secretaries, Arthur Bigge and Fritz Ponsonby (Henry Ponsonby had died in 1895), taught themselves to write in large, clear black script, but the queen asked them to write even larger and blacker. In spite of her blindness, giving up her official work was unthinkable. She still dealt with five or six government boxes of papers each day, though the letters were read aloud to her now. The Boer War roused her, as the Crimean War had done before. When she heard of the defeats of Black Week (December 1899), she declared: 'Please understand that there is no one depressed in this house; we are not interested in the possibilities of defeat; they do not exist.'[33] But Victoria felt the war acutely, and wept at the lists of casualties. She kept albums of the dead soldiers, and wrote letters to the widows of officers – in the opinion of one lady-in-waiting, it was this morbid work that killed her.[34]

Deaths crowded in on her. After the death in 1900 of

her son Alfred, Duke of Edinburgh, aged fifty-six of throat cancer, she lost her appetite entirely. She shrank to half her size and suffered tortures from insomnia – symptoms probably of an acute geriatric depression. The death of her thirty-three-year-old grandson Christle (Prince Christian Victor) from fever in South Africa was the final blow, plunging her into deepest melancholy. Severe depression probably hastened the cerebrovascular disease that killed her.[35]

As she lay dying at Osborne in January 1901, Lytton Strachey imagined her memories passing back and back into the distant past, to 'Albert's face under the green lamp ... and Lord M. dreaming at Windsor with rooks cawing in the elm trees, and the Archbishop of Canterbury on his knees in the dawn ... and her mother's feathers sweeping down towards her, and a great old repeater-watch of her father's in its tortoise-shell case, and a yellow rug, and some friendly flounces of sprigged muslin, and the trees and the grass at Kensington'.[36] But even on her deathbed Victoria was a monarch, aware of her dynastic duty to ensure the succession. The evening before she died, the semi-conscious queen asked for the Prince of Wales, the son with whom she had quarrelled for most of her life. 'Kiss my face,' she said. And she put out her arms, and said 'Bertie'. He embraced her and broke down.[37] With the death of the old queen, not only her family but also the nation had lost its mother.

Notes

INTRODUCTION

1. QV to Vicky, 23 December 1861, in *Dearest Mama*, ed. Roger Fulford (London: Evans Brothers, 1968), p. 26.
2. QV to Vicky, 18 December 1861, ibid., p. 23.
3. QV to Earl Canning, 10 January 1862, in *The Letters of Queen Victoria* [*QVL*], ed. A. C. Benson and Viscount Esher, vol. 3 (London: John Murray, 1908), p. 478.
4. QV to Earl Russell, 10 January 1862, in *The Letters of Queen Victoria: Second Series*, ed. G. E. Buckle, vol. 1 (London: John Murray, 1926), p. 10.
5. *'My Dear Duchess': Letters to the Duchess of Manchester*, ed. A. L. Kennedy (London: John Murray, 1956), p. 186.
6. QV to Leopold, 24 December 1861, in *QVL*, vol. 3, p. 476.
7. Lytton Strachey, *Queen Victoria* (London: Collins, 1958), p. 203.
8. Roger Fulford, *Hanover to Windsor* (London: Fontana, 1966), p. 38.
9. QV to Leopold, 17 February 1852, in *QVL*, vol. 2, p. 367.
10. Charles Moore, *Margaret Thatcher* (London: Allen Lane, 2013), p. xi.
11. QV to King Leopold, 20 December 1861, in *QVL*, vol. 3, p. 473.
12. QV to Alice, 12 January 1875, in Jane Ridley, *Bertie: A Life of Edward VII* (London: Chatto & Windus, 2012), p. 479.
13. Yvonne M. Ward, *Censoring Queen Victoria* (London: Oneworld, 2014).
14. Strachey, pp. 114, 198, 276.
15. Strachey to Vanessa Bell, 1 March 1919, in Michael Holroyd, *Lytton Strachey* (London: Vintage, 1995), p. 460.

1. 'A RESOLUTE LITTLE TIT'

1. RA VIC/MAIN/QVJ (W) [Queen Victoria's Journals online] 20 June 1837 (Lord Esher's typescripts).
2. Thomas Creevey to Miss Ord, 6 September 1837, *The Creevey Papers*, ed. Sir Herbert Maxwell (London: John Murray, 1912), p. 666.
3. Roger Fulford, *Royal Dukes* (London: Collins, 1973), pp. 164–81.
4. Monica Charlot, *Victoria: The Young Queen* (Oxford: Blackwell, 1991), pp. 32–3.
5. Cecil Woodham-Smith, *Queen Victoria* (London: Hamish Hamilton, 1972), p. 84. Kate Williams, *Becoming Queen* (London: Hutchinson, 2008), pp. 200–201.
6. Quoted in Charlot, p. 35.
7. Her sister-in-law, Louise of Gotha, in Richard Sotnick, *The Coburg Conspiracy* (London: Ephesus Publishing, 2008), p. 118.

8. Quoted in Charlot, p. 35.
9. Woodham-Smith, p. 75.
10. QV's 1872 note in *QVL*, vol. 1, p. 10.
11. Strachey, p. 41.
12. QV to Vicky, 9 June 1858, in *Dearest Child: Letters between Queen Victoria and the Princess Royal 1858–61*, ed. Roger Fulford (London: Evans Brothers, 1964), pp. 111–12.
13. RA VIC/MAIN/QVJ (W) 26 February 1838 (Lord Esher's typescripts).
14. Memo by Prince Charles Leiningen (QV's half-brother), 1841, in Woodham-Smith, p. 64. This is the definitive text on the Kensington system.
15. Diary of Susan Breeks, ed. Rosemary Blackett-Ord (to be published in 2015). RA VIC/MAIN/QVJ (W) 3 August 1833 (Lord Esher's typescripts).
16. A recent attempt to rehabilitate Conroy on the grounds that he believed that his wife was the illegitimate daughter of the Duke of Kent ignores the question of his dishonesty. A. N. Wilson, *Victoria* (London: Atlantic Books, 2014), pp. 34, 59–60. Woodham-Smith, pp. 256–60.
17. Charlot, p. 56.
18. QV to Bertie, 7 May 1859, in Ridley, *Bertie*, p. 46.
19. Anson's memo, 15 January 1841, in *QVL*, vol. 1, p. 256. Lynne Vallone, *Becoming Victoria* (New Haven and London: Yale University Press, 2001), pp. 40–42, 62–7.
20. Vallone, pp. 44–5.
21. Feodore to Duchess of Northumberland, V's official governess, 1836, in Ward, p. 95.
22. Woodham-Smith, p. 136.

2. CAMELOT

1. RA VIC/MAIN/QVJ (W) 28 June 1838 (Lord Esher's typescripts).
2. *Creevey Papers*, p. 664, 20 June 1837. Woodham-Smith, pp. 93–4.
3. *Creevey Papers*, p 668.
4. See Leopold to QV, 28 April 1837, 25 May 1837, 7 June 1837, 15 June 1837, 17 June 1837, 23 June 1837, 30 June 1837, in *QVL*, vol. 1, pp. 64–82.
5. Christopher Hibbert, *Queen Victoria: A Personal History* (London: HarperCollins, 2000), pp. 56–7.
6. RA VIC/MAIN/QVJ (W) 3 October 1837 (Lord Esher's typescripts).
7. Fulford, *Hanover to Windsor*, p. 44.
8. QV's memo to Ponsonby, 7 July 1872, in Ridley, *Bertie*, p. 160.
9. William M. Kuhn. *Henry and Mary Ponsonby* (London: Duckworth, 2002), p. 140. See Vernon Bogdanor, *The Monarchy and the Constitution* (Oxford: Clarendon Press, 1995), p. 199. Sir Robin Mackworth-Young, 'The Royal Archives', *Archives*, vol. 13 (1978), p. 119.
10. RA VIC/MAIN/QVJ (W) 2 February 1839 (Lord Esher's typescripts).
11. Lord Esher quoted in Ward, p. 98.
12. *The Greville Memoirs*, ed. Lytton Strachey and Roger Fulford, vol. 4 (London: Macmillan, 1938), vol. 4, p. 167, 12 May 1839.
13. Bogdanor, pp. 19–20.
14. Charlot, p. 137.
15. RA VIC/MAIN/QVJ (W) 5 July 1839 (Lord Esher's typescripts).

16. RA VIC/MAIN/QVJ (W) 21 June 1839 (Lord Esher's typescripts).
17. *Greville Memoirs*, vol. 4, p. 188, 7 July 1839.
18. Stockmar to Leopold, 19–23 February 1838, in Woodham-Smith, p. 163.

3. ALBERT

1. Quoted in Sotnick, p. 147. *Morning Chronicle*, 14 September 1824.
2. See Norman Davies's essay on Coburg in *Vanished Kingdoms* (London: Allen Lane, 2011), pp. 541–61.
3. Sotnick, pp. 16–35. Anthony Camp, *Royal Mistresses and Bastards* (privately printed, 2007), pp. 343–4.
4. Interview with Ulrike Grunewald, Coburg, 6 September 2013. See Ulrike Grunewald, *Luise Von Sachsen-Coburg-Saalfeld* (Cologne: Bohlau, 2013).
5. Memorandum by QV, in Hon. C. Grey, *The Early Years of the Prince Consort* (London: Smith, Elder, 1867), p. 17.
6. Memorandum by Christopher Florschutz, ibid., p. 92. Theodore Martin, *The Life of His Royal Highness the Prince Consort*, vol. 1 (London: Smith, Elder, 1875), p. 5. Karina Urbach, introduction to I. B. Taurus edn of Martin's *Life* (2012).
7. Memorandum by QV, in Grey, p. 24.
8. Memorandum by QV, ibid., pp. 17–18.
9. Memorandum by QV, ibid., p. 216.
10. Quoted ibid., p. 218.
11. RA VIC/MAIN/QVJ (W) 10, 11, 13, 14 October 1839 (Lord Esher's typescripts). Woodham-Smith, p. 183.
12. RA VIC/MAIN/QVJ (W) 15 October 1839 (Lord Esher's typescripts).
13. Philip Eade, *Young Prince Philip* (London: HarperPress, 2011), pp. 178–9.
14. Albert to Prince William of Lowenstein, 6 December 1839, in *Letters of the Prince Consort*, ed. Kurt Jagow (London: John Murray, 1938), p. 32.
15. Albert to QV, 30 November 1839, ibid., p. 30.
16. Woodham-Smith, p. 204.

4. THE TAMING OF THE SHREW

1. Jonathan Marsden, *Victoria and Albert: Art and Love* (Royal Collection, 2010), p. 67.
2. RA VIC/MAIN/QVJ (W) 11 February 1840 (Lord Esher's typescripts).
3. Marina Warner, *Queen Victoria's Sketchbook* (London: Macmillan, 1979), p. 59.
4. http://www.heraldica.org/topics/britain/prince_highness_docs.htm#1840. Albert's promotion from Serene Highness to Royal Highness leapfrogged the rank of Highness. My thanks to Glyn Redworth for advice on this point. Author emails, 24 September, 16 November, 22 November 2013.
5. QV to Albert, 31 January 1840, in *QVL*, vol. 1, p. 213. Albert to William Lowenstein, May 1840, in *Letters of the Prince Consort*, p. 69. Author email Patric Dickinson, 22 September 2014. Eade, p. 260.
6. Charlot, p. 193.

7. Anson's memo, 20 December 1840, in Woodham-Smith, p. 218.

8. Albert to Stockmar, 15 January 1842, in Charlot, p. 210.

9. RA VIC/MAIN/QVL (W) 15 January 1842 (Princess Beatrice's copies).

10. Albert to Stockmar, 18 January 1842, in Charlot, p. 211.

11. QV to Stockmar, 20 January 1842, ibid., p. 212. Woodham-Smith, p. 231.

12. QV to Theodore Martin, 18 February 1869, in QVL, 2nd series, vol. 1, p. 584.

13. Greville Memoirs, vol. 5, p. 129, 26 August 1843. Charlot, p. 232.

14. QV to Lady Canning, 10 January 1847, in Virginia Surtees, Charlotte Canning (London: John Murray, 1975), p. 172.

15. Margaret Homans, '"To the Queen's Private Apartments": Royal Family Portraiture and the Construction of Victoria's Sovereign Obedience', Victorian Studies, vol. 37 (1993), pp. 20-23. Richard Dorment, Telegraph, 23 March 2010.

16. Albert to Duke of Wellington, 6 April 1850, in Martin, vol. 2 (1876), p. 260.

17. E. S. Turner, The Court of St James's (Michael Joseph, 1959), pp. 305-8. See Stockmar's Memorandum on the Royal Household in Memoirs of Baron Stockmar, ed. Max Muller (Longmans, Green, 1873), vol. 2 pp. 118-25.

18. Grey, p. 354. Charlot, pp. 224-5. Turner, p. 308.

19. QV to Leopold, 4 April 1843, in QVL, vol. 1, p. 475. See Fulford, Hanover to Windsor, p. 61.

20. QV to Leopold, 29 October 1844, in QVL, vol. 2, p. 27.

21. QV to Leopold, 16 January 1844, in QVL, ibid., p. 5.

22. RA VIC/MAIN/QVJ (W) 8 February 1845 (Princess Beatrice's copies).

23. QV to Leopold, 25 March 1845, in QVL, vol. 2, p. 35.

24. QV to Melbourne, 3 April 1845, ibid., p. 36.

25. RA VIC/MAIN/QVJ (W) 30 July 1847 (Princess Beatrice's copies). Elizabeth Longford, Victoria R. I. (London: Weidenfeld & Nicolson, 1964), p. 211.

26. Charlotte Canning, in Kate Hubbard, Serving Victoria (London: Chatto & Windus, 2012), p. 111. RA VIC/MAIN/QVJ (W) 23 July 1845 (Princess Beatrice's copies).

27. Warner, pp. 108, 126-31.

28. Mark Girouard, Windsor (London: Hodder & Stoughton, 1993), p. 72. QV to Vicky, 20 March 1859, in Dearest Child, p. 169. Hubbard, p. 111.

29. QV to Vicky, 2 April 1859, in Dearest Child, pp. 170-71.

30. QV to Vicky, 16 March 1859, ibid., p. 167.

31. QV to Dowager Duchess of Saxe-Coburg-Gotha, 4 June 1840, in Charlot, p. 191.

32. QV to Leopold, 5 January 1841, in QVL, vol. 1, p. 255.

33. QV to Vicky, 24 March, 21 April, 15 June, 17 November 1858; 4 May 1859, in Dearest Child, pp. 77-8, 94, 115, 144, 191.

34. The Times, 18 November 1841.

35. QV to Princess Alice, 12 October 1864, in Hannah Pakula, An Uncommon Woman (London: Phoenix Press, 1997), p. 221. Valerie Fildes, Wet Nursing (Oxford: Basil Blackwell, 1988), pp. 190-204. Yvonne Ward, 'The Womanly Garb of Queen Victoria's Early Motherhood, 1840-42', Women's History Review, vol. 8 (1999).

36. QV to Vicky, 9 June 1858, in Dearest Child, p. 112.

37. QV to Vicky, 1 March 1858, ibid., p. 68.

38. Greville Memoirs, vol. 5, p. 98, 14 June 1843.

39. RA VIC M12/35, QV's Memo re Children's Education, 4 March 1844.

40. Warner, p. 133.

41. RA VIC/MAIN/QVJ (W) 10 June 1846 (Princess Beatrice's copies).

5. THE QUEEN'S MIND

1. RA VIC/MAIN/QVJ (W) 1 May 1851 (Princess Beatrice's copies).

2. QV to King Leopold, 3 May 1851, in *QVL*, vol. 2, p. 318.

3. Albert to Stockmar, 24 January 1854, in *Letters of the Prince Consort*, pp. 203–8. *Greville Memoirs*, vol. 7, pp. 4–9, January 1854. *Reynolds's Newspaper*, 25 December 1853. *Daily News*, 23 December 1853. Richard Williams, *The Contentious Crown* (Aldershot: Ashgate, 1997). Karina Urbach, 'Prince Albert and Lord Palmerston: Battle Royal', in *Prince Albert: A Wettin in Britain*, ed. Franz Bosbach and John R. Davis (Prince Albert Studies, vol. 22 [Munich, 2004]), pp. 83–93.

4. Stockmar to Albert, 22 January 1854, in Martin, vol. 2, pp. 545–57.

5. See David Cannadine, 'The Last Hanoverian Sovereign? The Victorian Monarchy in Historical Perspective, 1688–1988', in *The First Modern Society: Essays in Honour of Lawrence Stone*, ed. A. L. Beier, David Cannadine and James M. Rosenheim (Cambridge: Cambridge University Press, 1989), pp. 140–44. Bogdanor, pp. 23–4. John R. Davis, 'Liberalisation, the Parliamentary System and the Crown: The Role of Coburg Dynasties in the Nineteenth-Century Constitutional Debate', Prince Albert Society (forthcoming).

6. *Greville Memoirs*, vol. 7, pp. 306–7, 19 October 1857.

7. Sir Robin Mackworth-Young, *The Royal Archives and Prince Albert* (Prince Albert Society, Coburg, 1985). Sir Frederick Ponsonby, *Recollections of Three Reigns* (London: Odhams Press, n.d.), p. 67.

8. Strachey, p. 198.

9. *Derby, Disraeli and the Conservative Party: The Political Journals of Lord Stanley 1849–69*, ed. John Vincent (Hassocks: Harvester, 1978), p. 180.

10. QV to Leopold, 11 September 1855, in *QVL*, vol. 3, p. 142. RA VIC/MAIN/QVJ (W) 10 September 1855 (Princess Beatrice's copies).

11. Harry Ransom Centre, Lytton Strachey Papers, Strachey's note of interview with Lady Lytton, 15 July 1920.

12. QV to Leopold, 4 April 1848, in *QVL*, vol. 2, p. 167. QV to Leopold, 22 May 1855, in *QVL*, vol. 3, p. 127.

13. QV to Augusta, Princess of Prussia, 23 October 1854, in *Further Letters of Queen Victoria*, ed. Hector Bolitho (London: Thornton Butterworth, 1938), p. 51. Walter L. Arnstein, 'The Warrior Queen: Reflections on Victoria and her World', *Albion*, vol. 30 (1998), pp. 8–14.

14. Ronald W. Clark, *Balmoral* (London: Thames & Hudson, 1981). Hubbard, p. 122.

15. Albert to Duchess Marie of Saxe-Coburg, 22 September 1844, in *Letters of the Prince Consort*, p. 95.

16. Jane Ridley, '"The Sport of Kings": Shooting and the Court of Edward VII', *Court Historian*, vol. 18 (2013), pp. 190–93. Duff Hart-Davis, *Monarchs of the Glen* (London: Cape, 1978), pp. 109–20.

17. RA VIC/Add T2/90, QV to Bertie, 16 October 1859.

18. RA VIC/MAIN/QVJ (W) 29 April 1859 (Princess Beatrice's copies).

19. Albert to QV, 5 November 1856, in Woodham-Smith, p. 330.

20. Albert to QV, 2 May 1853, 16 November 1855, ibid., pp. 329–30.

21. Royal College of Physicians, Diary of Sir James Clark, 5 February 1856.

22. *Greville Memoirs*, vol. 7, p. 388, 12 December 1858.

23. Ida Macalpine and Richard Hunter, *George III and the Mad Business* (London: Allen Lane, 1969). John C. G. Rohl, Martin Warren and David Hunt, *Purple Secret* (London: Corgi, 1999) claim that Victoria inherited porphyria and passed it on to some of her children. Timothy Peters, 'King George III, Bipolar Disorder, Porphyria and Lessons for Historians', *Clinical Medicine*, vol. 11 (2011), pp. 261–4. Timothy Peters and Clive Willis, 'Mad Monarchs', *Court Historian*, vol. 19 (2014), pp. 29–42.

24. QV to Vicky, 9 June 1858, in *Dearest Child*, p. 111.

25. Memorandum by QV, May 1856, in *QVL*, vol. 3, pp. 192–4.

26. QV's notebook, 'Remarks – Conversations – Reflections', 10 February 1859, in Longford, p. 283.

27. RA VIC/Z261/89–91, QV's 'Remarks – Conversations – Reflections', 30 December 1858.

28. Albert to QV, 22 October 1861, in Longford, p. 292.

29. Ibid., p. 273.

30. See Hibbert, p. 410 n.

31. QV's Reminiscences, January 1862, in Woodham-Smith, p. 332.

32. QV to Vicky, 24 March 1858, 11 June 1858, in *Dearest Child*, p. 112. QV to Vicky, 8 September 1862, in *Dearest Mama*, pp. 105–6.

33. QV to Augusta of Prussia, 6 October 1856, in *Further Letters*, p. 75.

34. *Greville Memoirs*, vol. 7, p. 388, 12 December 1858. Albert to QV, 1 October 1856, in Woodham-Smith, p. 330.

35. *Dearest Child*, p. 138 n.

36. QV to Leopold, 9 February 1858, in *QVL*, vol. 3, p. 264.

37. QV to Vicky, 26 May 1858, in *Dearest Child*, p. 108.

38. *Greville Memoirs*, vol. 7, pp. 387–9. *Dearest Child*, pp. 135–8.

39. QV to Vicky, 6, 7 February 1858, in *Dearest Child*, pp. 32, 24.

40. Fulford introduction, ibid., pp. 6–11.

41. RA VIC/Z261/50–7, QV's 'Remarks – Conversations – Reflections', 2 May 1858.

42. Albert to Stockmar, 6 January 1846, in *Letters of the Prince Consort*, p. 99. Cannadine, 'Last Hanoverian', pp. 44–5.

43. Ridley, *Bertie*, pp. 21–7, 32–3, 41–4.

44. RA VIC/Add T1/183, QV to Bertie, 26 August 1857.

45. QV to Vicky, 27 April 1859, in *Dearest Child*, p. 187. Ridley, *Bertie*, p. 27.

46. QV to Vicky, 27 November 1858, in *Dearest Child*, p. 147.

47. QV's 'Remarks – Conversations – Reflections,' 2 May 1858, in Ridley, *Bertie*, p. 40.

6. ALONE

1. RA VIC/MAIN/QVJ (W) 2–7 December 1861 (Princess Beatrice's copies). Martin, vol. 5 (1880), pp. 417, 428–32. QV to Leopold, 6 December 1861, in *QVL*, vol. 3, p. 471.

2. Martin, vol. 5, p. 439.

3. See *The Times*, 21, 30 December 1861.

4. Helen Rappaport, *Magnificent Obsession* (London: Hutchinson, 2011), pp. 249–60. J. W. Paulley, 'The Death of Albert Prince Consort: The Case Against Typhoid Fever', *Quarterly Journal of Medicine*, vol. 86 (1993), pp. 837–41.

5. QV to Vicky, 13 February, 27 November 1861, in *Dearest Child*, pp. 308, 370. QV to Vicky, 27 December 1861, in *Dearest Mama*, p. 30.

6. QV to Vicky, 12 November 1862, in *Dearest Mama*, p. 132.
7. Albert to Bertie, 16 November 1861, in Woodham-Smith, p. 416.
8. RA VIC/Add MSS U/16, Lord Hertford's Account of Queen Victoria, 12 February 1862.
9. QV to Vicky, 27 December 1861, in *Dearest Mama*, p. 30. Ridley, *Bertie*, p. 71.
10. Fulford, *Hanover to Windsor*, p. 83.
11. R. Williams, p. 206.
12. *Derby, Disraeli*, p. 183.
13. QV to Russell, 10 January 1862, in *QVL*, 2nd series, vol. 1, p. 9.
14. RA VIC/Add MSS U/16, Lord Hertford's Account of Queen Victoria, 12 February 1862.
15. QV to Vicky, 2 May 1862, in *Dearest Mama*, p. 59.
16. QV to Queen Augusta of Prussia, 16 December 1862, 26 September 1863, in *Further Letters*, p. 129. Warner, p. 193.
17. QV to Augusta, 26 September 1863, in *Further Letters*, p. 145. QV to Vicky, 8 September 1862, in *Dearest Mama*, pp. 105–6.
18. Colin Murray Parkes, *Bereavement* (London: Penguin, 1986), p. 126. Pat Jalland, *Death in the Victorian Family* (Oxford: Oxford University Press, 1996), pp. 318–21. I am grateful to Anthony Mann for advice on grief.
19. Charlot, pp. 410–12. Wilson, pp. 245–7. 'My Dear Duchess', p. 148.
20. QV to Leopold, 16 June 1863, in *QVL*, 2nd series, vol. 1, p. 91.
21. QV to Vicky, 3 December 1862, in *Dearest Mama*, p. 145.
22. Longford, p. 321.
23. *The Times*, 6 April 1864.
24. QV to Russell, 8 December 1864, in *QVL*, 2nd series, vol. 1, pp. 244–5.
25. Roy Jenkins, *Gladstone* (London: Papermac, 1996), p. 243.
26. Grey to Charles Phipps, 4 September 1863, in Peter Arengo-Jones, *Queen Victoria in Switzerland* (London: Robert Hale, 1995), p. 18.
27. QV to Russell, 22 January 1866, in *QVL*, 2nd series, vol. 1, p. 296.
28. RA VIC/MAIN/QVJ (W) 6 February 1866 (Princess Beatrice's copies). *The Times*, 7 February 1866. Anna Keay, *The Crown Jewels* (London: Thames & Hudson, 2011), pp. 158–61.
29. QV to Vicky, 11 January 1862, in *Dearest Mama*, p. 37.
30. Palmerston to QV, 14 December 1861, in Kuhn, p. 148.
31. QV to Theodore Martin, 19 January 1868, in Theodore Martin, *Queen Victoria as I Knew Her* (London: William Blackwood, 1908), p. 29.
32. 'My Dear Duchess', p. 183.
33. QV to Grey, 15 February 1862, in Kuhn, p.149.
34. QV to King Leopold, 25 February 1864, in *QVL*, 2nd series, vol. 1, p. 168.
35. Frederick Ponsonby, pp. 67–8.
36. 'My Dear Duchess', p. 248

7. MRS BROWN

1. Tom Cullen, *The Empress Brown* (London: Bodley Head, 1969), p. 225.
2. QV to Vicky, 11 August 1866, in *Your Dear Letter*, ed. Roger Fulford (London: Evans Brothers, 1971), p. 90.
3. *Derby, Disraeli*, pp. 232, 248.

4. According to Lord Norwich, writing in the *Oldie*, Steven Runciman alleged that Victoria not only married John Brown but also had children by him (Michael Thornton in the *Daily Mail*, 25 February 2012). Dorothy Thompson, *Queen Victoria: Gender and Power* (London: Virago, 1990), pp. 61–87.

5. *Derby, Disraeli*, pp. 247–8, 16 March 1866.

6. Raymond Lamont-Brown, *John Brown* (Stroud: Sutton, 2000), p. 70.

7. Arthur Ponsonby, *Henry Ponsonby* (London: Macmillan, 1942), p. 126. Frederick Ponsonby, p. 22.

8. Oliver Millar, *The Victorian Pictures in the Collection of Her Majesty the Queen: Text* (Cambridge: Cambridge University Press, 1992), p. 147. Cullen, pp. 100–104.

9. *Derby, Disraeli*, p. 313, 30 June 1867.

10. QV to Lord Charles Fitzroy, 20 July 1867, in *QVL*, 2nd series, vol. 1, pp. 449–50.

11. Arthur Helps in introduction to Queen Victoria, *Leaves from the Journal of Our Life in the Highlands* (London: Smith Elder, 1868), p. ix.

12. Hibbert, pp. 329–30. *My Mistress the Queen: The Letters of Frieda Arnold Dresser to Queen Victoria*, ed. Benita Stoney and Heinrich C. Weltzien (London: Weidenfeld & Nicolson, 1994), p. 25.

13. RA VIC/Z448/186, QV to Bertie, 7 January 1868. See *Derby Diaries, 1869–78*, ed. John Vincent (London: Royal Historical Society, 1994), p. 178, 30 August 1874.

14. Fitzwilliam Museum, Wilfrid Blunt Papers, MS 33-1975, Diary, 18 August 1885; MS 9-1975, 4 June 1909.

15. *Loulou: Selected Extracts from the Journal of Lewis Harcourt*, ed. Patrick Jackson (Madison, N J: Farleigh Dickinson University Press, 2006), pp. 81–2, 17 February 1885.

16. Cullen, p. 227.

17. *Derby Diaries*, pp. 416, 474, 9 July and 30 December 1877.

18. Wilson, p. 421.

19. *Henry Ponsonby*, p. 129.

20. Bendor Grosvenor, 'Dear John', *History Today*, vol. 55 (2005).

21. Victoria's Instructions for my Dressers to be Opened Directly after my Death, 9 December 1897, quoted in Wilson, p. 555.

22. Ibid., p. 554.

23. *Henry Ponsonby*, p. 128.

24. *Advice to a Grand-daughter*, ed. Richard Hough (London: Heinemann, 1975), p. 45, QV to Victoria of Hesse, 3 April 1883. See Wilson, pp. 311–27.

8. DEAREST MAMA

1. Charlotte Zeepvat, *Queen Victoria's Youngest Son* (London: Thistle, 2013), pp. 18–21, 27, 75–6. QV to Vicky, 5 February 1873, in *Darling Child*, ed. Roger Fulford (London: Evans Brothers, 1976), pp. 75–6.

2. RA VIC/MAIN/QVJ (W) 4 February 1868 (Princess Beatrice's copies).

3. Zeepvat, pp. 67–8, 78, 85.

4. QV to Vicky, 11 April 1868, in *Your Dear Letter*, p. 184.

5. Zeepvat, pp. 82, 118.

6. Balliol College, Oxford, Harold Nicolson Diary, 6 January 1949.

7. QV to Alice, 7 July 1863, in Ridley, *Bertie*, p. 79.

8. Quoted in *Dearest Mama*, p. 12.
9. *'My Dear Duchess'*, p. 189.
10. Rappaport, p. 120. Wilson, p. 269.
11. Matthew Dennison, *The Last Princess* (London: Weidenfeld & Nicolson, 2007), pp. 26–9, 37.
12. QV to King Leopold, 18 May 1863, in *QVL*, 2nd series, vol. 1, p. 85.
13. QV to Vicky, 2 July 1862, in *Dearest Mama*, p. 85.
14. QV to Alice, 14 May 1863, in Ridley, *Bertie*, p. 79.
15. QV to Vicky, 23 December 1865, in *Your Dear Letter*, p. 50.
16. QV to Lord Granville, 18/19 October 1870, in Jehanne Wake, *Princess Louise* (London: Collins, 1988), p. 130. Wake gives a superbly well-researched account of Victoria's matchmaking for Louise.
17. QV to Bertie, 29 November 1869, in *QVL*, 2nd series, vol. 1, pp. 632–3.
18. QV to Vicky, 25 October 1878, in *Darling Child*, p. 65. See Cannadine, 'Last Hanoverian', pp. 151–2.
19. Quoted in Longford, p. 395.
20. QV to Vicky, 29 November 1881, in *Beloved Mama*, ed. Roger Fulford (London: Evans Brothers, 1981), p. 112. See Zeepvat, pp. 228–34.
21. QV to Vicky, 20 October 1873, in *Darling Child*, p. 112.
22. Giles St Aubyn, *Queen Victoria* (London: Sinclair-Stevenson, 1991), p. 219.

9. THE FAERY: GLADSTONE AND DISRAELI

1. Gladstone to Granville, 1 October 1871, in *The Political Correspondence of Mr Gladstone and Lord Granville*, ed. Agatha Ramm (London: Royal Historical Society, 1952), vol. 2, p. 266.
2. QV to Lord Hatherley, Lord Chancellor, 10 August 1871, in Philip Guedalla, *The Queen and Mr Gladstone*, vol. 1 (London: Hodder & Stoughton, 1933), pp. 299–300.
3. Gladstone to Ponsonby, 16 August 1871, ibid., p. 304.
4. Grey to Gladstone, 1 and 5 June 1869, ibid., pp. 52–3. Kuhn, p. 152.
5. *Henry Ponsonby*, p. 134.
6. Hibbert, p. 339. Longford, p. 91.
7. William M. Kuhn, 'Queen Victoria's Civil List: What Did She Do With It?', *Historical Journal*, vol. 36 (1993), pp. 645–65.
8. 'The Illness of the Prince of Wales', in *Collected Works of Walter Bagehot*, ed. Norman St John-Stevas (London: The Economist, 1974), vol. 5, pp. 435–6.
9. QV to Gladstone, 22 January 1872, in Guedalla, p. 329.
10. QVJ, 27 February 1872, in *QVL*, 2nd series, vol. 2, p. 195.
11. QV to Gladstone, 29 February 1872, in Guedalla, p. 338.
12. QV to Ponsonby, 5 July 1872, in Ridley, *Bertie*, p. 160. Gladstone to QV, 5 July 1872, in Guedalla, pp. 351–9.
13. QV to Gladstone, 12 July 1872; Gladstone to QV, 17 July 1872; QV to Gladstone, 2 September 1872, in Guedalla, pp. 359–66, 379.
14. Jenkins, p. 332. I am grateful to Vernon Bogdanor for advice on QV's relations with Gladstone and Disraeli.
15. Guedalla, p. 47.

16. Bogdanor, p. 34.
17. QV to Vicky, 24 February 1874, in *Darling Child*, p. 130.
18. *Henry Ponsonby*, pp. 134–5.
19. Disraeli to QV, 26 February 1868, in *QVL*, 2nd series, vol. 1, p. 505.
20. Disraeli to wife, 28 February 1868, in W. F. Monypenny and G. E. Buckle, *Life of Benjamin Disraeli*, vol. 2 (London: John Murray, 1929), p. 326.
21. QV to Vicky, 4 March 1868, in *Your Dear Letter*, p. 176.
22. QV to Vicky, 26, 29 February 1868, ibid., p. 174.
23. Robert Blake, *Disraeli* (London: Eyre & Spottiswoode, 1966), p. 492.
24. QV's memo, 20 February 1874, in *QVL*, 2nd series, vol. 2, p. 323.
25. Disraeli to Lady Bradford, 7 August, 12 September 1874, in Monypenny and Buckle, pp. 679, 685.
26. Ibid., p. 1335.
27. Blake, p. 490.
28. *Henry Ponsonby*, p. 245.
29. Disraeli to QV, 25 February 1875, in Monypenny and Buckle, p. 1336.
30. *Henry Ponsonby*, p. 245.
31. *Derby Diaries*, pp. 196, 202 (17, 27 February 1875).
32. Derby to Disraeli, 4 May 1874, in Monypenny and Buckle, p. 754. Bogdanor, pp. 37–8. *Derby Diaries*, pp. 369, 431.
33. *Henry Ponsonby*, p. 141.
34. QV to Disraeli, 10 January 1878, in Monypenny and Buckle, p. 1089.
35. QV to Vicky, 15 February 1878, in *Darling Child*, p. 282.
36. Monypenny and Buckle, p. 1022. Longford, p. 412.
37. QV to Disraeli, 9 April 1880, in Monypenny and Buckle, p.1399.
38. QV to Vicky, 24 March, 5 April 1880, in *Beloved Mama*, pp. 71, 73.
39. QV to Henry Ponsonby, 4 April 1880, in *Henry Ponsonby*, p. 184.
40. QV to Henry Ponsonby, 8 April 1880, in *QVL*, 2nd series, vol. 3, p. 76.
41. Jenkins, pp. 438–9. QV's Memo, 23 April 1880, in *QVL*, 2nd series, vol. 3, p. 85.
42. QV to Disraeli, 23 April 1880, in Monypenny and Buckle, p. 1411.
43. QV to Vicky, 2 May 1880, in *Beloved Mama*, p. 78.
44. *Diary of Sir Edward Walter Hamilton*, ed. Dudley Bahlman, vol. 1 (Oxford: Clarendon Press, 1972), p. 49, 11 September 1880.
45. Jenkins, pp. 468–70.
46. QV to Ponsonby, 31 May 1882, in *Henry Ponsonby*, p. 192.
47. *QVL*, 2nd series, vol. 3, p. 177.
48. QV to Ponsonby, 30 May 1892; QVJ, 15 August 1892, in *QVL*, 3rd series, vol. 2, pp. 120, 145.
49. Guedalla, vol. 2, p. 76.
50. Bogdanor, p. 32.

10. GRANDMAMA V. R. I.

1. According to one account, the queen delivered this rebuke to Alick Yorke, equerry and amateur actor-producer at court, when he told a risqué story. *Life with Queen*

Victoria: Marie Mallet's Letters from Court 1887–1901, ed. Victor Mallet (London: John Murray, 1968), p. xiii.

2. Ibid., e.g. pp. 40, 44, 47, 61, 122.
3. Harry Ransom Centre, Lytton Strachey Papers, Strachey's note of interview with Lady Lytton, 15 July 1920.
4. Frederick Ponsonby, pp. 13, 22. *Life with Queen Victoria*, p. 204.
5. Consuelo Vanderbilt Balsan, *The Glitter and the Gold* (London: William Heinemann, 1953), p. 87.
6. Marie of Romania quoted in Greg King, *Twilight of Splendor* (Hoboken N J: John Wiley, 2007), p. 104.
7. This passage from 1883 was not included in Davidson's published diaries. Quoted in Andrew Roberts, *Salisbury* (Weidenfeld & Nicolson, 1999), p. 318.
8. Michael Nelson, *Queen Victoria and the Discovery of the Riviera* (London: I. B. Tauris, 2001), p. 26. *Life with Queen Victoria*, p. 47.
9. R. Williams, p. 134.
10. QV's memo, 8 February 1886, in *Letters of Queen Victoria*, 3rd series, vol. 1, p. 46.
11. Longford, pp. 485–92. Roberts, p. 377.
12. Roberts, p. 793. *Life with Queen Victoria*, p. 101.
13. QV to Vicky, 6 July 1892, in Longford, p. 518.
14. Lord David Cecil, *The Cecils of Hatfield House* (London: Constable, 1973), p. 249. Longford, p. 567.
15. *The Times*, 22 June 1887.
16. David Cannadine, 'The Context, Performance and Meaning of Ritual: The British Monarchy and the "Invention of Tradition", c.1820–1977', in *The Invention of Tradition*, ed. Eric Hobsbawm and Terence Ranger (Cambridge: Cambridge University Press, 1983). But see Walter L. Arnstein, 'Queen Victoria Opens Parliament: The Disinvention of Tradition', *Historical Research*, vol. 63 (1990), esp. pp. 190–91.
17. Benedict Anderson, *Imagined Communities* (London: Verso, 1991), p. 88.
18. QVJ, 21 June 1887, in *QVL*, 3rd series, vol. 1, p. 324.
19. *Gladstone Diaries*, ed. H. C. G. Matthew, vol. 12 (Oxford: Clarendon Press, 1994), p. 45 (21 June 1887).
20. Anderson, pp. 19–22. See Jane Ridley, '"Europe's Grandmother": Queen Victoria and her German Relations', Prince Albert Society (forthcoming).
21. QV to Vicky, 26 April 1876, in *Darling Child*, p. 209.
22. *Advice to a Grand-daughter*, p. 29.
23. *Advice to a Grand-daughter*, pp. 29, 56, 82, 26, 126.
24. QV to Vicky, 5 February 1853, in *Darling Child*, pp. 75–6. Zeepvat, pp. 18–21.
25. *Advice to a Grand-daughter*, pp. 116–17.
26. *A King's Story: The Memoirs of H.R.H. the Duke of Windsor* (London: Cassell, 1951), p. 9.
27. Balliol College, Oxford, Harold Nicolson Diary, 27 July 1949.
28. *Queen Victoria at Windsor and Balmoral: Letters from her Grand-daughter Princess Victoria of Prussia, June 1899*, ed. James Pope-Hennessy (London: Allen and Unwin, 1959), p. 69.
29. *Advice to a Grand-daughter*, p. 65.
30. RA VIC/MAIN/QVJ (W) 25 February 1885 (Princess Beatrice's copies).
31. Longford, pp. 546–8.
32. HRC, Strachey Papers, Lady Lytton interview, 15 July 1920. *Henry Ponsonby*, p. 359.

33. Longford, p. 554.
34. HRC, Strachey Papers, Lady Lytton interview, 15 July 1920. Frederick Ponsonby, pp. 75–9.
35. Robert C. Abrams, 'Late-life Depression and the Death of Queen Victoria', *International Journal of Geriatric Psychiatry*, vol. 25 (2010).
36. Strachey, p. 281.
37. Ridley, *Bertie*, p. 342.

Further Reading

There was no official biography of Queen Victoria. Lytton Strachey's *Queen Victoria* (London: Collins, 1958) is still worth reading – brilliantly written, with an uncanny ability to be right in spite of using no unpublished papers. The first biography based on sources in the Royal Archives was Elizabeth Longford's *Victoria R. I.* (London: Weidenfeld & Nicolson, 1964). This broke new ground by opening up Victoria's private life, and it is still the best full biography. Cecil Woodham-Smith published only one volume of a projected two-volume life, but her *Queen Victoria* (London: Hamish Hamilton, 1972) is indispensable as a quarry. Monica Charlot's *Victoria: The Young Queen* (Oxford: Blackwell, 1991) was the first biography to document Prince Albert's search for power, but this too stops in 1861. Christopher Hibbert's *Queen Victoria: A Personal History* (London: HarperCollins, 2000) is useful. A. N. Wilson's *Victoria* (London: Atlantic Books, 2014) stresses Victoria's German links and shines light on the years of her widowhood.

Victoria was a prolific diarist, writing an estimated average of 2,000 words every day of her life. Her digitalized journals can all be read online at http://www.queenvictoriasjournals.org/home.do This superb resource hosts the handwritten copies of Victoria's journals made by her daughter Princess Beatrice. Beatrice redacted the journals, omitting material that she considered sensitive, trivial or upsetting to family members, and she destroyed the originals as she went. Also on this site is the typescript commissioned by Lord Esher of the journals 1832–40. This is a complete transcript of the originals; the section of

Victoria's journals covering the period from her accession in 1837 to her marriage in 1840 is especially fascinating.

After Victoria's death the decision was made to commemorate her in her own words, by publishing a selection of her letters. *The Letters of Queen Victoria* edited by A. C. Benson and Lord Esher, 3 vols (London: John Murray, 1908) cover the years 1837–61. A further six official volumes followed, edited by G. E. Buckle. *The Letters of Queen Victoria: Second Series,* 3 vols (London: John Murray, 1926–8) take the story up to 1885, and *The Letters of Queen Victoria: Third Series,* 3 vols (London: John Murray, 1930–32) continue to 1901. Philip Guedalla's *The Queen and Mr Gladstone,* 2 vols (London: Hodder & Stoughton, 1933) prints letters from Victoria which were considered too outspoken for inclusion in the official edition.

After the formality of Queen Victoria's official correspondence, the publication of her letters to her daughter Vicky, later Empress of Germany, came as a sensation. The letters – frank, forthright and intensely human – begin in 1858, with Vicky's marriage to Fritz, heir to the King of Prussia. They form the key text for modern biographies of Victoria. Victoria's letters escaped the royal editors because they were kept in Germany, at Vicky's house at Friedrichshof, near Kronberg. In 1945 the Americans commandeered Friedrichshof, and King George VI sent out the royal librarian, Sir Owen Morshead, to bring the letters back to Windsor. Five volumes of the so-called Kronberg letters from 1858 to 1885 were edited by Roger Fulford: *Dearest Child* (London: Evans Brothers, 1964), *Dearest Mama* (London: Evans Brothers, 1968), *Your Dear Letter* (London: Evans Brothers, 1971), *Darling Child* (London: Evans Brothers, 1976), and *Beloved Mama* (London: Evans Brothers, 1981). Also valuable are Victoria's letters to Princess Victoria of Hesse, *Advice to a Grand-daughter,* edited by Richard Hough (London: Heinemann, 1975).

The young Victoria was the subject of the 2009 film of that name as well as Kate Williams's *Becoming Queen* (London: Hutchinson, 2008). On Victoria's education, see Lynne Vallone, *Becoming Victoria* (New

Haven and London: Yale University Press, 2001), and for Conroy and the Kensington system, see Katherine Hudson, *A Royal Conflict* (London: Hodder & Stoughton, 1994). Yvonne M. Ward's *Censoring Queen Victoria* (London: Oneworld, 2014) gives a critique of Benson and Esher's editorial policy, showing how their selection of letters was designed to construct an image of the young queen. For Albert's death and its consequences, see Helen Rappaport, *Magnificent Obsession* (London: Hutchinson, 2011). Marina Warner's *Queen Victoria's Sketchbook* (London: Macmillan, 1979) is full of insight.

Albert's official biography was directed by Victoria. *The Early Years of the Prince Consort* by the Hon. C. Grey (London: Smith, Elder, 1867) is largely composed of memoirs that Victoria wrote after Albert's death. Theodore Martin's monumental *Life of His Royal Highness the Prince Consort*, 5 vols (London: Smith, Elder, 1875–80) was written under close supervision by the queen. Modern biographies include Robert Rhodes James's *Albert, Prince Consort* (London: Hamish Hamilton, 1983) and Stanley Weintraub's *Albert: Uncrowned King* (London: John Murray, 1997), but the definitive life is yet to be written. The Prince Albert Society has generated important research on royal Anglo-German links. See especially *Royal Kinship: Anglo-German Family Networks 1815–1918*, edited by Karina Urbach (Munich: Prince Albert Society, 2008). Norman Davies's *Vanished Kingdoms* (London: Allen Lane, 2011) contains a stimulating essay on Rosenau.

There are several lives of Victoria's children. For Bertie, see Philip Magnus, *King Edward VII* (London: John Murray, 1964) and Jane Ridley, *Bertie: A Life of Edward VII* (London: Chatto & Windus, 2012). Vicky's life has been written by Hannah Pakula, *An Uncommon Woman* (London: Phoenix Press, 1997). Jehanne Wake's *Princess Louise* (London: Collins, 1988) is still the best biography of this princess. For Beatrice, see Matthew Dennison, *The Last Princess* (London: Weidenfeld & Nicolson, 2007). Charlotte Zeepvat's *Queen Victoria's Youngest Son* (London: Thistle, 2013) documents Leopold's haemophilia.

Insider comment on the Victorian court is often the most revealing. Henry Ponsonby and his family were shrewd and humorous observers of their mistress. See *Henry Ponsonby* by his son Arthur Ponsonby (London: Macmillan, 1942); Frederick Ponsonby, *Recollections of Three Reigns* (London: Odhams Press, n.d.); and William M. Kuhn's engaging *Henry and Mary Ponsonby* (London: Duckworth, 2002). Michaela Reid's *Ask Sir James* (London: Eland, 1996) is the diary of Victoria's doctor Sir James Reid – royal doctors (and royal dogs) got closer to monarchs than anyone. *Life with Queen Victoria: Marie Mallet's Letters from Court 1887–1901*, edited by Victor Mallet (London: John Murray, 1968) and *Lady Lytton's Court Diary*, edited by Mary Lutyens (London: Hart-Davis, 1961), are two ladies-in-waiting's accounts of the last years of Victoria's court. See also Kate Hubbard, *Serving Victoria* (London: Chatto & Windus, 2012) and Martyn Downer, *The Queen's Knight* (London: Bantam Press, 2007). For John Brown, there is Tom Cullen, *The Empress Brown* (London: Bodley Head, 1969) and Raymond Lamont-Brown, *John Brown* (Stroud: Sutton, 2000).

The modern historical debate about Queen Victoria begins with two seminal articles by David Cannadine: 'The Context, Performance and Meaning of Ritual: The British Monarchy and the "Invention of Tradition", *c.*1820–1977', in *The Invention of Tradition*, edited by Eric Hobsbawm and Terence Ranger (Cambridge: Cambridge University Press, 1983); and 'The Last Hanoverian Sovereign? The Victorian Monarchy in Historical Perspective, 1688–1988', in *The First Modern Society: Essays in Honour of Lawrence Stone*, edited by A. L. Beier, David Cannadine and James M. Rosenheim (Cambridge: Cambridge University Press, 1989). Walter L. Arnstein, 'Queen Victoria Opens Parliament: The Disinvention of Tradition', *Historical Research*, vol. 63 (1990) is a response. See also Walter L. Arnstein, 'The Warrior Queen: Reflections on Victoria and her World', *Albion*, vol. 30 (1998). For Victoria's finances, see William M. Kuhn, 'Queen Victoria's Civil List: What Did She Do With It?', *Historical Journal*, vol. 36 (1993).

Margaret Homans, '"To the Queen's Private Apartments": Royal Family Portraiture and the Construction of Victoria's Sovereign Obedience', *Victorian Studies*, vol. 37 (1993) explores the queen's cultural significance. *The Monarchy and the British Political Nation*, edited by Andrzej Olechnowicz (Cambridge: Cambridge University Press, 2007) is a valuable collection of essays.

Vernon Bogdanor, *The Monarchy and the Constitution* (Oxford: Clarendon Press, 1995) is definitive. Roger Fulford's *Hanover to Windsor* (London: Fontana, 1966) has a thoughtful essay on Queen Victoria. Richard Williams's *The Contentious Crown* (Aldershot: Ashgate, 1997) explores public attitudes towards the Victorian monarchy. See also Frank Prochaska's *Royal Bounty: The Making of a Welfare Monarchy* (New Haven and London: Yale University Press, 1995), and Sir Oliver Millar, *The Victorian Pictures in the Collection of Her Majesty the Queen*, 2 vols (Cambridge: Cambridge University Press, 1992).

Picture Credits

1. Thomas Sully, portrait of Queen Victoria, 1838 (The Wallace Collection, London/Bridgeman Images)
2. Franz Winterhalter, portrait of Queen Victoria, 1843 (Royal Collection Trust © Her Majesty Queen Elizabeth II, 2014/ Bridgeman Images)
3. Sir William (Charles) Ross, portrait of Prince Albert, 1840 (Royal Collection Trust © Her Majesty Queen Elizabeth II, 2014/Bridgeman Images)
4. Franz Winterhalter, *The Royal Family in 1846* (Royal Collection Trust © Her Majesty Queen Elizabeth II, 2014/Bridgeman Images)
5. John Mayall, carte-de-visite of Queen Victoria and Prince Albert, 1861 (Royal Collection Trust © Her Majesty Queen Elizabeth II, 2014)
6. Baron Heinrich von Angeli, portrait of Queen Victoria, 1877 (Christie's/Bridgeman Images)
7. Queen Victoria, 'View from my window at Balmoral by moonlight, October 1864', watercolour sketch (Royal Collection Trust © Her Majesty Queen Elizabeth II, 2014)
8. Sir Edwin Landseer, *Queen Victoria at Osborne*, 1867 (Royal Collection Trust © Her Majesty Queen Elizabeth II, 2014/ Bridgeman Images)
9. Unknown photographer, Queen Victoria and Abdul Karim, 'the Munshi', 1897 (The Illustrated London News Picture Library/ Bridgeman Images)

10. Laurits Tuxen, *The Family of Queen Victoria in 1887* (Royal Collection Trust © Her Majesty Queen Elizabeth II, 2014/ Bridgeman Images)
11. Laurits Tuxen, portrait of Queen Victoria, 1894 (The Hirschsprung Collection, Copenhagen, Denmark/akg-images)

Acknowledgements

My greatest debt is to Stuart Proffitt, a prince among editors, who asked me to write this book. I have found Queen Victoria to be an endlessly fascinating subject. 'We authors, Ma'am,' Disraeli is said to have remarked to Victoria, and she was far more of an author than he could possibly have imagined. Her copious writings are a biographer's goldmine. I should like to thank Her Majesty Queen Elizabeth II for permission to quote from the papers of Queen Victoria in the Royal Archives at Windsor. I am grateful to Pam Clark for her guidance. My visit to Coburg for the Prince Albert Society Conference in September 2013 opened my eyes to Albert's family background. Thanks to Vernon Bogdanor, Clarissa Campbell-Orr, Patric Dickinson, Anthony Mann, Glynn Redpath and Andrew Wilson. At Penguin, Anna Hervé, Donald Futers, Linden Lawson and Cecilia Mackay have done a superb job. Caroline Dawnay, my agent, has been a wonderful friend both to me and to this book. My son Toby read and made valuable comments on the manuscript. Special thanks to both Toby and Humphrey for putting up with me, even in my Queen Victoria moments.

Index

Penguin Monarchs

THE HOUSES OF WESSEX AND DENMARK

Athelstan*	Tom Holland
Aethelred the Unready	Richard Abels
Cnut	Ryan Lavelle
Edward the Confessor	

THE HOUSES OF NORMANDY, BLOIS AND ANJOU

William I*	Marc Morris
William II	John Gillingham
Henry I	Edmund King
Stephen	Carl Watkins
Henry II*	Richard Barber
Richard I	Thomas Asbridge
John	Nicholas Vincent

THE HOUSE OF PLANTAGENET

Henry III	Stephen Church
Edward I*	Andy King
Edward II	Christopher Given-Wilson
Edward III*	Jonathan Sumption
Richard II*	Laura Ashe

THE HOUSES OF LANCASTER AND YORK

Henry IV	Catherine Nall
Henry V*	Anne Curry
Henry VI	James Ross
Edward IV	A. J. Pollard
Edward V	Thomas Penn
Richard III	Rosemary Horrox

* Now in paperback

THE HOUSE OF TUDOR

Henry VII	Sean Cunningham
Henry VIII*	John Guy
Edward VI*	Stephen Alford
Mary I*	John Edwards
Elizabeth I	Helen Castor

THE HOUSE OF STUART

James I	Thomas Cogswell
Charles I*	Mark Kishlansky
[Cromwell*	David Horspool]
Charles II*	Clare Jackson
James II	David Womersley
William III & Mary II*	Jonathan Keates
Anne	Richard Hewlings

THE HOUSE OF HANOVER

George I	Tim Blanning
George II	Norman Davies
George III	Amanda Foreman
George IV	Stella Tillyard
William IV	Roger Knight
Victoria*	Jane Ridley

THE HOUSES OF SAXE-COBURG & GOTHA AND WINDSOR

Edward VII*	Richard Davenport-Hines
George V*	David Cannadine
Edward VIII*	Piers Brendon
George VI*	Philip Ziegler
Elizabeth II*	Douglas Hurd

* Now in paperback

ALLEN LANE
an imprint of
PENGUIN BOOKS

Also Published

Jordan B. Peterson, *12 Rules for Life: An Antidote to Chaos*

Bruno Maçães, *The Dawn of Eurasia: On the Trail of the New World Order*

Brock Bastian, *The Other Side of Happiness: Embracing a More Fearless Approach to Living*

Ryan Lavelle, *Cnut: The North Sea King*

Tim Blanning, *George I: The Lucky King*

Thomas Cogswell, *James I: The Phoenix King*

Pete Souza, *Obama, An Intimate Portrait: The Historic Presidency in Photographs*

Robert Dallek, *Franklin D. Roosevelt: A Political Life*

Norman Davies, *Beneath Another Sky: A Global Journey into History*

Ian Black, *Enemies and Neighbours: Arabs and Jews in Palestine and Israel, 1917-2017*

Martin Goodman, *A History of Judaism*

Shami Chakrabarti, *Of Women: In the 21st Century*

Stephen Kotkin, *Stalin, Vol. II: Waiting for Hitler, 1928-1941*

Lindsey Fitzharris, *The Butchering Art: Joseph Lister's Quest to Transform the Grisly World of Victorian Medicine*

Serhii Plokhy, *Lost Kingdom: A History of Russian Nationalism from Ivan the Great to Vladimir Putin*

Mark Mazower, *What You Did Not Tell: A Russian Past and the Journey Home*

Lawrence Freedman, *The Future of War: A History*

Niall Ferguson, *The Square and the Tower: Networks, Hierarchies and the Struggle for Global Power*

Matthew Walker, *Why We Sleep: The New Science of Sleep and Dreams*

Edward O. Wilson, *The Origins of Creativity*

John Bradshaw, *The Animals Among Us: The New Science of Anthropology*

David Cannadine, *Victorious Century: The United Kingdom, 1800-1906*

Leonard Susskind and Art Friedman, *Special Relativity and Classical Field Theory*

Maria Alyokhina, *Riot Days*

Oona A. Hathaway and Scott J. Shapiro, *The Internationalists: And Their Plan to Outlaw War*

Chris Renwick, *Bread for All: The Origins of the Welfare State*

Anne Applebaum, *Red Famine: Stalin's War on Ukraine*

Richard McGregor, *Asia's Reckoning: The Struggle for Global Dominance*

Chris Kraus, *After Kathy Acker: A Biography*

Sayeeda Warsi, *The Enemy Within: A Tale of Muslim Britain*

Alexander Betts and Paul Collier, *Refuge: Transforming a Broken Refugee System*

Robert Bickers, *Out of China: How the Chinese Ended the Era of Western Domination*

Erica Benner, *Be Like the Fox: Machiavelli's Lifelong Quest for Freedom*

William D. Cohan, *Why Wall Street Matters*

David Horspool, *Oliver Cromwell: The Protector*

Daniel C. Dennett, *From Bacteria to Bach and Back: The Evolution of Minds*

Derek Thompson, *Hit Makers: How Things Become Popular*

Harriet Harman, *A Woman's Work*

Wendell Berry, *The World-Ending Fire: The Essential Wendell Berry*

Daniel Levin, *Nothing but a Circus: Misadventures among the Powerful*

Stephen Church, *Henry III: A Simple and God-Fearing King*

Pankaj Mishra, *Age of Anger: A History of the Present*

Graeme Wood, *The Way of the Strangers: Encounters with the Islamic State*

Michael Lewis, *The Undoing Project: A Friendship that Changed the World*

John Romer, *A History of Ancient Egypt, Volume 2: From the Great Pyramid to the Fall of the Middle Kingdom*

Andy King, *Edward I: A New King Arthur?*

Thomas L. Friedman, *Thank You for Being Late: An Optimist's Guide to Thriving in the Age of Accelerations*

John Edwards, *Mary I: The Daughter of Time*

Grayson Perry, *The Descent of Man*

Deyan Sudjic, *The Language of Cities*

Norman Ohler, *Blitzed: Drugs in Nazi Germany*

Carlo Rovelli, *Reality Is Not What It Seems: The Journey to Quantum Gravity*

Catherine Merridale, *Lenin on the Train*

Susan Greenfield, *A Day in the Life of the Brain: The Neuroscience of Consciousness from Dawn Till Dusk*

Christopher Given-Wilson, *Edward II: The Terrors of Kingship*

Emma Jane Kirby, *The Optician of Lampedusa*

Minoo Dinshaw, *Outlandish Knight: The Byzantine Life of Steven Runciman*

Candice Millard, *Hero of the Empire: The Making of Winston Churchill*

Christopher de Hamel, *Meetings with Remarkable Manuscripts*

Brian Cox and Jeff Forshaw, *Universal: A Guide to the Cosmos*

Ryan Avent, *The Wealth of Humans: Work and Its Absence in the Twenty-first Century*

Jodie Archer and Matthew L. Jockers, *The Bestseller Code*

Cathy O'Neil, *Weapons of Math Destruction: How Big Data Increases Inequality and Threatens Democracy*

Peter Wadhams, *A Farewell to Ice: A Report from the Arctic*

Richard J. Evans, *The Pursuit of Power: Europe, 1815-1914*

Anthony Gottlieb, *The Dream of Enlightenment: The Rise of Modern Philosophy*

Marc Morris, *William I: England's Conqueror*

Gareth Stedman Jones, *Karl Marx: Greatness and Illusion*

J.C.H. King, *Blood and Land: The Story of Native North America*

Robert Gerwarth, *The Vanquished: Why the First World War Failed to End, 1917-1923*

Joseph Stiglitz, *The Euro: And Its Threat to Europe*

John Bradshaw and Sarah Ellis, *The Trainable Cat: How to Make Life Happier for You and Your Cat*

A J Pollard, *Edward IV: The Summer King*

Erri de Luca, *The Day Before Happiness*

Diarmaid MacCulloch, *All Things Made New: Writings on the Reformation*

Daniel Beer, *The House of the Dead: Siberian Exile Under the Tsars*

Tom Holland, *Athelstan: The Making of England*

Christopher Goscha, *The Penguin History of Modern Vietnam*

Mark Singer, *Trump and Me*

Roger Scruton, *The Ring of Truth: The Wisdom of Wagner's Ring of the Nibelung*

Ruchir Sharma, *The Rise and Fall of Nations: Ten Rules of Change in the Post-Crisis World*

Jonathan Sumption, *Edward III: A Heroic Failure*

Daniel Todman, *Britain's War: Into Battle, 1937-1941*

Dacher Keltner, *The Power Paradox: How We Gain and Lose Influence*

Tom Gash, *Criminal: The Truth About Why People Do Bad Things*

Brendan Simms, *Britain's Europe: A Thousand Years of Conflict and Cooperation*

Slavoj Žižek, *Against the Double Blackmail: Refugees, Terror, and Other Troubles with the Neighbours*

Lynsey Hanley, *Respectable: The Experience of Class*

Piers Brendon, *Edward VIII: The Uncrowned King*

Matthew Desmond, *Evicted: Poverty and Profit in the American City*

T.M. Devine, *Independence or Union: Scotland's Past and Scotland's Present*

Seamus Murphy, *The Republic*

Jerry Brotton, *This Orient Isle: Elizabethan England and the Islamic World*

Srinath Raghavan, *India's War: The Making of Modern South Asia, 1939-1945*

Clare Jackson, *Charles II: The Star King*

Nandan Nilekani and Viral Shah, *Rebooting India: Realizing a Billion Aspirations*

Sunil Khilnani, *Incarnations: India in 50 Lives*

Helen Pearson, *The Life Project: The Extraordinary Story of Our Ordinary Lives*

Ben Ratliff, *Every Song Ever: Twenty Ways to Listen to Music Now*

Richard Davenport-Hines, *Edward VII: The Cosmopolitan King*

Peter H. Wilson, *The Holy Roman Empire: A Thousand Years of Europe's History*

Todd Rose, *The End of Average: How to Succeed in a World that Values Sameness*